Study Skills for Early Years Students

Alison Mitchell

Hodder & Stoughton

A MEMBER OF THE HODDER HEADLINE GROUP

Orders: please contact Bookpoint Ltd, 78 Milton Park, Abingdon, Oxon OX14 4TD. Telephone: (44) 01235 827720, Fax: (44) 01235 400454. Lines are open from 9.00–6.00, Monday to Saturday, with a 24 hour message answering service. Email address: orders@bookpoint.co.uk

British Library Cataloguing in Publication Data
A catalogue record for this title is available from The British Library

ISBN 0 340 780 827

First published 2001
Impression number   10 9 8 7 6
Year   2005 2004 2003 2002

Cover illustration by Debbie Tonge
Typeset by Fakenham Photosetting Ltd., Fakenham, Norfolk.
Printed in Great Britain for Hodder & Stoughton Educational, a division of Hodder Headline Plc, 338 Euston Road, London NW1 3BH by J. W. Arrowsmith Ltd., Bristol

Contents

Introduction

Anyone who says they managed to gain their qualification without doing any studying is teasing you. If you want to do well, you will need to set aside time to study. You will also need to be motivated and be able to use your time well.

Five simple steps to good studying
1 Take time to study on a regular basis.
2 Use your time effectively.
3 Settle down to your studies quickly e.g. leave that phone call to your friend until after you have finished your work.
4 Find a good place to study.
5 Use a study method that works for you.

The purpose of this book is to help you to improve your study skills and prepare you for the different methods of assessment that you may have to complete while working towards your qualification. However, this book will not write the assignment for you or revise for examinations. You have to do that.

Finding your way around each chapter
Each chapter follows the same format.

1 Aims
   Each chapter begins by outlining the aims of the chapter and headings are provided to direct you to specific topics.
2 Activities
   Activities are provided throughout the chapter to help you to find ways of improving your study skills. Some of these activities you will need to do on your own but it is more fun to do them with a friend and share your answers.

Before you begin to read this book, answer the questions on the following page. There is no time limit, but be honest with yourself.

ACTIVITY

How good are your study skills? Complete the checklist below to find out your strengths and weakness.

	Yes	No	Sometimes

The best way to learn

1 Do you enjoy learning?
2 Are you happy with your study routine?
3 Can you study despite the distractions around you?
4 Can you find information from your study notes when you want to?
5 Do you decide what you want to study and keep to your plan?

Finding information

6 Do you find it easy to find the books you want in the library?
7 Can you find information on the Internet quickly and easily?
8 Do you use a range of text books when preparing for your assignments?

Writing assignments

9 Do you understand the difference between the words – describe, explain, evaluate, account for?
10 Do you find it easy to write the first paragraph of your assignment?

Preparing for examinations

11 Do you write a detailed timetable when preparing for examinations and keep to it?
12 Do you prefer examinations rather than writing assignments?
13 Do you answer the questions that you are confident about first?

	Yes	No	Sometimes
Giving an oral presentation			
14 Are you confident when speaking in public?			
15 Have you prepared an oral presentation before?			
16 Do you enjoy taking part in group discussions?			
Building a portfolio			
17 Do you know what a portfolio is?			
18 Do you enjoy working on projects?			
19 Are you good at disciplining yourself to complete work by a set date?			
20 Do you enjoy gathering information from different sources?			
Total			

When you have finished the checklist, add up each column to show you where your main strengths and weaknesses are in relation to study skills and what areas you will need to focus on.

Acknowledgements

I would like to thank Joan Gillian for her valuable contribution to Chapter 2 and the support that she has given me throughout the writing of the book. I would also like to thank Mum, Dad and Ian for their constant prodding and Elizabeth for her endless patience over the last few months.

I would also like to take this opportunity to thank the early years tutors up and down the country who have contributed indirectly to the development of the materials in this book.

The cartoons used in the book were drawn by Martin Berry.

1

The Most Effective Way to Learn

The aim of this chapter is to help you:

- identify your own learning style
- use different ways of recording information
- use different strategies that will make your learning more effective.

Learning is a process that goes on throughout our lives and it is very personal to each one of us in terms of our own interests and needs. We learn by looking, listening, experimenting and building on past experiences. Learning should be stimulating and challenging. However, sometimes it can be a painful process which is anything but enjoyable. We can all remember a time in our lives when learning something new was extremely difficult and took a long time e.g. learning to drive a car for the first time or trying to understand the process of long division.

Adults who work with young children need to understand how young children learn and how they themselves learn, to ensure that they provide the most effective opportunities for individual children to practise and develop new skills and understand concepts.

> Adults who enjoy learning and being with children are much more likely to provide a high quality early childhood setting for children and their families.
>
> Bruce, T and Meggit, C (1996:59)

This chapter considers the most effective way of learning but it does not attempt to explain the complex process of how young children learn.

Effective learning

Did you know that:

- music can aid learning;

- if you are too hot or too cold your learning will not be as effective;
- you were born with approximately 100 billion brain cells;
- the brain is less than 2% of your body weight and without oxygen it does not function;
- your brain needs sufficient sleep to function effectively;
- your brain needs food and drink (but not alcohol!)?

While working towards your qualification you will find out how children learn, but do you know how you learn best?

ACTIVITY

Read each of the descriptions and decide who you are most like?

- Visual Vera
- Practical Pete
- Auditory Abdul

Visual Vera's work area is neat and tidy. She plans ahead but tends to day dream and doodle instead of listening carefully. She has a good visual memory and likes her lessons to have diagrams, overheads and illustrations. She tends to say phrases like 'That looks right to me' or 'I can see what you mean'.

Practical Pete never sits still and always fidgets. He uses a lot of gestures when talking. He enjoys making things and remembers things best by doing. Pete speaks quite slowly and often says 'Run that by me' and 'I'll handle that' or 'I feel at home with this idea'.

Auditory Abdul likes listening to rhyme and rhythm. He talks to himself but is easily distracted by noise. Abdul is good at chatting, discussing and debating and prefers to spell out loud. His phrases are 'Sounds good to me' and 'That rings a bell'.

Using the checklist below, tick off the learning strategies that Vera, Abdul and Pete might use, then do the same task for yourself to find out whether you are a visual learner, an auditory learner or a tactile learner?

	Vera	Abdul	Pete	Yourself
highlighting				
talking through the task				
using cartoons, diagrams				
talking out loud				
taping key facts				
discussing with others				
making a game of the key facts				
moving around while learning				
playing music while studying				
using a tape to summarise passages				
using post-its to summarise notes				
drawing mind maps or spider charts				
using different colours when making notes				
imaging yourself doing the task that is being explained				

Now that you have identified how you learn best, you can begin to find out your most effective ways of studying.

Finding the right time

- Everyone is different. Some people prefer to study first thing in the morning while others prefer to work at night. You need to find out the time that is best for you.

- The most effective studying is often done in short chunks but take care that the chunks do not become so short that you are not studying at all. We can all come up with good excuses to avoid studying. The maximum 'on task' time for adults is approximately 20–25 minutes with breaks of 2–5 minutes in between. Always allow more time if you know that the subject is difficult.

Finding the right environment

- Everyone has his or her own preferences. Some people prefer to work in the college library while others prefer their own room at home. A lot will depend on the number of distractions that you are likely to get while studying e.g. mobile phone, family interruptions.
- Make sure that the room temperature is appropriate i.e. not too hot (or you may fall asleep) and not too cold as you will become very uncomfortable.
- Always try to have a suitable work surface to work at and a chair that is of the right height. Your neck and back can become very stiff if your table and chair are not suitable. Sitting at a desk is better than lying on your bed.
- Music can aid learning. In the past, total silence was often considered to be the only way to study effectively. However you may prefer to have music on in the background but take care that it is not too 'wordy' or you will soon become distracted.

Reward yourself

If you feel you have done well, give yourself a treat. Meet up with friends, go shopping or do things that you have been putting off to allow you to study. You are more likely to go back to studying if you know there is a reward at the end of the task.

ACTIVITY

Read the statements below and tick the ones you think are essential for your learning.

1 a quiet room
2 coffee to stimulate the brain
3 a mobile phone to keep in contact with your friends
4 a hi-fi system
5 good lighting and heating
6 water
7 a 'do not disturb' sign on the door
8 regular meetings with friends on the same course
9 a computer, internet, CD Rom
10 adequate sleep
11 appropriate text books, notes, paper, pencils, highlighting pens etc.
12 plenty of sunshine
13 regular breaks and exercise i.e. every fifteen minutes
14 a good table and chair that are at an appropriate height
15 regular meals

Discuss your answers with your friends. Some of the statements will be essential for you but not for your friends and vice versa.

Managing your time

Managing your time means achieving the end result within the time given. Planning your time is not an activity that you complete for one assignment. It is a process that involves several activities at the same time and goes on throughout your course and after you have qualified.

ACTIVITY

Susan has recently started an early years course and has been working in a day nursery for four weeks, as part of her work placement. Ahmed, the nursery manager has asked Susan to prepare the painting area in preparation for the next day. He has specifically asked her to cut the paper into different shapes and choose new colours of paint for the children to work with the next day. Susan wants to leave the nursery on time because she needs to buy a birthday card and present for her boy friend. The shop closes half an hour after her shift at the nursery finishes.

When the children leave the nursery, Susan begins to work on the creative area. She puts all the waste materials into the bucket and washes the surfaces. Jo, the nursery nurse asks Susan if she would like a drink and she agrees. She spends the next ten minutes in the staff room.

When Susan returns to the painting area, she begins to lay the children's paintings out in the storage area. She notices that there is only twenty minutes before her shift finishes. Susan begins to wash the paint pots but has great difficulty because the paint is sticking to the sides of the pots. She continues to scrape the pots and eventually they are almost clean. Susan puts the same colours of paints into the pots that had been used that day. She puts the paper that had been left over from the afternoon session into the storage racks. Susan leaves the nursery and finds that the shop has shut. She is very angry and blames Ahmed for asking her to do such a big task on her own.

1 Why did Susan forget to cut out the paper into different shapes?
2 Why did Susan not get to the shop on time?
3 Will Ahmed be happy with the job that Susan has done? Give reasons for your answer.
4 Was Susan right to blame Ahmed?
5 Could Susan have started with a different task first?
6 What could Susan have done to make sure that the task was done well and still have time to buy the birthday card and present for her boyfriend?

When you are planning your time do you:

- write effective notes;
- prioritise the tasks that you need to do i.e. do the most important tasks first;
- take account of how long a task will take and how much time you have to do the task in;
- blame others if you do not get the task done on time.

Ten questions to ask yourself before you begin to plan your time

1 What do I need to do?
2 When do I need to have it finished?
3 What could stop me from achieving it?
4 When can I start?
5 When should I start?
6 What is the most important task that I must do?
7 Who can help me complete the task?
8 Who can encourage me to finish the task?
9 How can I make sure that I am meeting my targets?
10 What could wait until another time?

Managing your time when preparing assignments is essential. It is very easy to panic when you are given assignments to do by a set date as you often think that you do not have enough time. The situation appears to get worse when you go to your next class and are given another piece of work to hand in for assessment by a specific date.

When you feel overwhelmed by the amount of work that you need to do, it is essential to prioritise your work.

ACTIVITY

How well do you manage your time? Complete the following questionnaire and find out how well you scored.

	Often	Sometimes	Rarely
1 Do you write daily to-do lists?			
2 Do you prioritise your to-do lists according to which items have the highest pay off for you?			
3 Do you finish all the tasks on your to-do list?			
4 Do you regularly update your personal goals, in writing?			
5 Is your desk clean and organised?			
6 Do you put everything in its place?			
7 Do you deal effectively with interruptions?			
8 Can you easily find items in your files?			
9 Are you assertive?			
10 Do you allow yourself quiet time during which you can work undisturbed every day?			
11 Are you able to cut-short unimportant phone calls?			
12 Do you focus on preventing problems before they arise rather than solving them after they happen?			
13 Do you make the best use of your time?			
14 Do you meet deadlines with time to spare?			
15 Are you on time to college and work?			
16 Do you delegate well?			
17 Do others co-operate enthusiastically on projects you are working on?			
18 When you are interrupted, can you return to your work without losing momentum?			

	Often	Sometimes	Rarely
19 Do you do something every day that moves you nearer to your long-term goal?			
20 Can you relax during your free time without worrying about your work?			
21 Do people know the best time to reach you?			
22 Do you do your most important work during your energy peak hours?			
23 When working on group projects, could others carry on most of your responsibilities if you were not there?			
24 Do you finish assignments on time?			
25 Do you handle each piece of paperwork only once?			

Source: Unknown

Give yourself **4** points for every 'often' you ticked.
Give yourself **2** points for every 'sometimes' you ticked.
Give yourself **0** points for every rarely.
Add your points together and compare yourself with the scale below.

81–100 You manage your time well. You are in control of most situations.
61–80   You manage your time well some of the time. However, you need to be more consistent with time-saving strategies your are already using.
41–60   You are slipping! Do not let circumstances get the better of you.
21–40   You are losing control! You are probably too disorganised to enjoy any quality time.
0–20   You are overwhelmed, scattered, frustrated and most likely under a lot of stress right now.

After you have completed the activity on 'Managing your time', make a list of the areas you would like to change.

In a few weeks time, complete the questionnaire again to see if you have improved your time management skills.

The Do's and Don'ts of managing your time

- Take notes that you can refer to easily.
- Ask questions if you do not understand the task. It is likely that you are not the only person who does not understand.
- Date your notes and make sure that you give a relevant title for each class.
- File your notes and handouts in such a way that you can find the information quickly. Dividers are very useful to separate different topics.
- Try to avoid re-writing notes. This takes up a lot of time and do you really learn from the task?
- Re-read your notes whenever you have a spare moment e.g. travelling to college.
- Use your study periods effectively. Do not be tempted to go shopping or chat with your friends.
- Do not take on too many extra activities while you are studying. You will get too tired and it will be difficult to find time to study or prepare for assessments.

Managing your time when writing assignments or preparing for examinations

1 Write down all the tasks that you have to do.
2 Prioritise the tasks.
3 Block time out in your diary in order to achieve the tasks.
4 Be realistic in your target setting to ensure success.
5 Arrange to do unpleasant tasks in between the enjoyable tasks.
6 Set yourself short term and long-term targets.
7 Do one job at a time.
8 Build in 'crises' point into your timetabling, e.g. Computers have a tendency to freeze the night before you are due to hand in your assignment.
9 Share your concerns with a friend or your tutor.
10 Make sure you have time to relax.

ACTIVITY

When you are given as assignment to complete, it can be helpful to create a time plan. One way of doing this is to start at the end and work backwards!

Complete the table on page 12 when you are given your first assignment. Remember to take account of work commitments and social events that you have already arranged. (You may find that you have to cancel some in order to give yourself enough time to complete the assignment.)

Tasks to be completed	Date
• Read assignment and brain storm ideas (This could be done with other students but remember that the work you hand in *must* be your own.) • Gather information and make notes • Plan your assignment • Begin first draft of assignment • Attend assignment workshop • Proof read it and add or amend information • Word process or handwrite your final copy (Allow plenty of time for this task as it can take a long time. Remember that if you are word processing your assignment, computers have a tendency to freeze the day before you hand in your work.) • Make a list of where to find information. This could include possible books, magazines, internet etc. • Proof read and spell check your work for the last time • Hand in your work on time or before if possible	

Completing this task can be quite daunting as you suddenly realise that there is not as much time to complete the assignment as you first thought. However, the more often you do this type of planning the more skilled you will become at it.

The time plan may be used for each assignment as the process does not change, however you may find it helpful to adapt the time plan for your own purposes.

ACTIVITY

You have been given the following tasks to complete by the end of term, which is in 6 weeks' time:

- a written observation of a child in your work placement;
- an assignment for your unit on 'Work with Babies';
- revision for a final examination.

Discuss with a colleague how you could plan your time over the next few weeks, to ensure that all the work is completed within six weeks.

Coping with stress

Everyone will feel stressed at some stage during their studies. This can be due to a number of different factors, e.g.:

- disputes with parents, friends, partners or tutors;
- victimisation, bullying, cliques, gangs, personal threats, low self esteem, lack of self confidence, negative self talk;
- inability to connect learning with personal goals or values;
- belief that the work is too difficult; inability to make a beginning on tasks;
- inability to understand the connections between current and past or possible future learning;
- physical or intellectual difficulty in accessing material as presented;
- poor sight or hearing;
- distractions in the learning environment;
- poor self management and study skills.

(Smith, A. 1998)

ACTIVITY

Are you stressed?

	Yes	No
1 You find it difficult to concentrate.		
2 You are short tempered.		
3 You are easily startled by small sounds.		
4 You feel queasy and suffer from indigestion.		
5 You are not interested in food.		
6 You never stop eating, particularly sweet things.		
7 You seem to have a constant headache.		
8 You want to cry at the silliest of things or run away from people particularly in large crowds.		
9 You are smoking more.		
10 One minute you are really happy and the next you feel really down.		

The more 'yes's' the more stress!

Becoming less stressed

If you feel under stress, it is important to find out what is causing the stress and do something about it before the situation gets any worse. It may be helpful to discuss your difficulties with your personal tutor. He or she can provide advice or suggest others who can give support.

- Talk the situation over with your personal tutor. He/she may be able to provide advice or suggest others who can give more support.
- Set realistic goals. Accept that there are some tasks that you will not be able to do because you do not have the time.
- Relax. Have some time off from your studies. Go to the gym, go for a walk, meet up with friends who are not on the course.
- Avoid alcohol, pills and too much caffeine as this does not solve the problem and may create others.
- Make sure you are getting enough sleep. Being tired can make matters worse.

2

Finding Information

The aim of this chapter is to help you:

- find the type of information that may be needed to complete the task
- identify different sources where information may be found
- reference information
- read effectively
- write effective notes.

Finding the right information is an essential task for anyone working towards a qualification, but if you do not know where to look for that information it can be very time consuming.

Storing and retrieving information

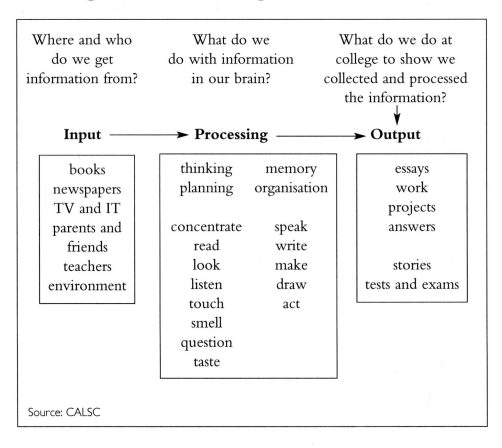

Where and who do we get information from?	What do we do with information in our brain?	What do we do at college to show we collected and processed the information?
Input →	**Processing** →	**Output**
books newspapers TV and IT parents and friends teachers environment	thinking memory planning organisation concentrate speak read write look make listen draw touch act smell question taste	essays work projects answers stories tests and exams

Source: CALSC

Different sources

Information can be gained from a wide range of sources including:

- Learning resource centres/libraries e.g. books, journals
- Media e.g. television, radio, video, newspapers
- Information technology e.g. Internet, CD ROM, DVD
- Professional organisations e.g. National Children's Bureau, Early Education (BAECE)
- Local services, e.g. Health Board, Social Services, Local Government Offices, Citizens Advice Bureaux.

Finding appropriate books in the Learning Resource Centre

Finding information related to early education may be difficult because it covers a wide range of subjects. Relevant information may be found in the under the following subject areas in the learning resource centre:

- Education
- Psychology
- Health, medicine, nursing
- Child-care
- Management
- Social science
- Curriculum areas e.g. physical education, environmental studies, art, music etc.

To help you find an appropriate book, most learning resource centres use the Dewey Decimal Classification System. Numbers are used to help you find the appropriate section. The main subject areas are listed below.

000	Generalities
100	Philosophy and Psychology
200	Religion
300	Social Sciences
400	Language
500	Natural Science and Mathematics
600	Technology (Applied Sciences)
700	The Arts Fine and Decorative Arts
800	Literature and Rhetoric
900	Geography and History

If you are looking for a specific book it is helpful to look up the cataloguing system. If you are not sure how to use it, ask the staff in the learning resource centre.

More information about the Dewey Classification System can be found on the Internet. www.oclc.org/oclc/fp

ACTIVITY

Using the Dewey Classification System, what subject would you find the following topics in? Check your answers by visiting the Learning Resource Centre.

Topic	Subject area	Classification Number
Cognitive development of young children Immunisation programmes Language and literacy in the early years Poverty Child protection procedures Physical care of babies		

Remember that you may find information about a topic in more than one subject area.

Journals, Newspapers, Government Reports

The Learning Resource Centre will also have copies of relevant journals, newspapers, government reports and statistics. The list below is a small sample of appropriate materials. Add to your list as you find more.

Resources	Title
Journals	Child Education
	Nursery Projects
	Nursery World
	Nursery Topics
	Childcare Quarterly
	(Kids Club Network)
	Co-ordinate
	(National Early Years
	Network)
Newspaper	Guardian (Tuesday)
	Times Educational
	Supplement (Friday)
Government	Department for Education
reports	and Employment
	Qualification and
	Curriculum Authority
	Department of Health

Back copies of newspapers are stored on CD Roms. Ask the Learning Resource Centre staff for help in using them.

ACTIVITY

You have been asked to find information on three different topics. Copy and complete the table below. You may find that you cannot obtain information from some of the sources. Compare your answers with a colleague and add to your information.

	Topics		
	Outdoor Play	Healthy Eating	Meningitis
Newspapers Note the name of the newspaper, the date and page of the article, the title of the article and author.			
Journals Note the name of the journal, the year, and journal number, the page of the article, the author's name and title of the article			
CD Rom Note the title of the CD Rom and the page number			
Internet addresses Note the full address, the page number and the date you noted the information			
Census data Note the year, topic, sources whether it is the internet or book			
Statistics Note the source Internet, CD Rom or books			
Books Note the author, initial, year of publication, title of book, place of publication and publisher			
Any other source			

Once you have found useful information you will need to read it carefully. If the material belongs to you then you can highlight the information but if the material is borrowed then you will need to make notes. Remember to make a note of the source of your information, as you will need it for the bibliography.

After reading the text, it is useful to summarise what you have read to make sure you have fully understood the information by drawing a mind map or using index cards. By doing this, you may find that you have not fully understood the information and it may be appropriate to reread the information again.

Finding information in books

Most tutors will provide you with a book list at the beginning of each unit. If they recommend that you buy specific books then it is worth spending the money. However if you are given a long list of books do not buy them all. This is very expensive and you should be able to borrow them from the learning resources centre or local library.

It is not possible to read every book that is available on a specific topic, however it is important to be able to select relevant books quickly and easily. Although it will not work every time, the following hints should make it easier.

1 Look at the front cover of the book. This can often give you an indication of the relevance of the book.
2 Read the summary that has been provided by the publisher. This may be on the back cover of the book or inside on the first few pages.
3 The contents page will provide an overview of the topics in the book.
4 The index will provide more specific information.

ACTIVITY

A Level 3 Early Years student has been given the following assignment to work on.

An early years worker is concerned that a child in the nursery is being physically abuse.
a) Describe the possible signs of physical abuse.
b) What procedures should the nursery have to manage such situations?
c) Give a brief description of the child protection procedures outlined in the Children Act 1989.

1 Information from the front cover

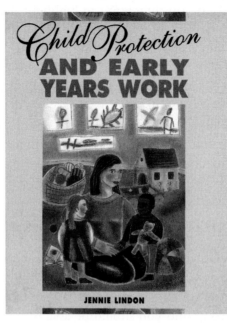

Using the information on the front cover of the book, do you think that it may help the student complete the task?

2 Publisher's summary

An understanding of child protection is part of good practice for all early years settings. Workers and students who have regular contact with children and families have a central role to play because of their knowledge of and concern for individual children. Yet, if unprepared, early years workers can find themselves on the sidelines of child protection, uncertain about the best action to take.

Child Protection and Early Years Work provides information, practical advice and case studies that will help you to:

- Learn about the broad framework of child protection, including legislation and how your work contributes to the bigger picture
- Understand the different kinds of child abuse and warning signs that should concern you
- Develop an informed and confident role as an early years worker: what you can do and what you should pass on to other professionals
- Work well with children and families where there is a child protection concern
- Establish essential good practice in partnership with parents, observation and record keeping
- Consider issues of equal opportunities and child protection.

Jennie Lindon is a Chartered Psychologist who has worked extensively with services for children and their families. She has published many books and articles, including Working with Young Children (Hodder and Stoughton).

The publisher usually includes a summary of the book either on the back cover, or inside the front page of the book. This can provide valuable information without having to read the whole book.

Having read the publisher's information, do you think the book is useful for the student? Will the book provide sufficient information for the student? Highlight the key words that you have helped you make your decision.

3 Contents Page

Using the information from the first page of the contents, suggest the chapters and relevant pages that the student might look at to help find the relevant information for each question.

	Relevant Chapter	Pages
Question 1		
Question 2		
Question 3		

4 Index

Using the index at the back of the book can provide much more specific information. The page numbering can also give useful information e.g. if there is a range of numbers indicated e.g. non-accidental injury 101–103, it indicates that there is detailed information provided. However if a series of numbers are provided e.g. NSPCC 42,43 it indicates that there may be a sentence or short paragraph.

Complete the table below.

Key words	Relevant pages in book
signs	
physical abuse	
policies	
procedures	
protection	

Were you able to find all the relevant pages? If not, what would you suggest that the student does next?

Before you borrow the book or return it to the shelf, it is always useful to look at the bibliography to see how extensive the author's sources are. It is also useful to flick through the book. If it is mainly text with very few diagrams, charts, illustrations etc will you ever read the book?

• Other facts to consider when choosing the right book

When was the book published? It may be giving you information that is out of date.

Where was it published? Some aspects of child-care and education are very specific to Britain.

Which book would be best for your assignment? Give reasons for your answer.

1 First published 1993
Fourth impression 2000

2 First published 1993
Reprinted 2000

3 First published USA 1993
Second impression UK 2000

Using the Internet to find information

There is a great deal of rubbish on the web but there is good information too. You need therefore to know the best ways to search for the good information.

Below are some ways to search for information.

1 Using addresses
2 Using search engines
3 Using key words

1 Using addresses

If you know the address of the organisation that you wish to look up, then this can be typed in the location or address space at the top of the screen. It must be copied exactly.

Addresses usually begin with http:// You do not need to type this in the location space as your computer will add this information automatically.

All addresses follow a similar format i.e.

www.childcare-info.co.uk

www	world wide web
childcare-info	company name
co	type of company
uk	country

Web site address	Explanation of Sites
www.piaget.org	org stands for an organisation. There is no country listed so the web site is in the USA.
www.childcare-info.co.uk	co stands for a company and the UK is the country.
www.niss.ac.uk	ac stands for academic, usually a college or university
www.dfee.gov.uk	gov stands for a government web site in Britain
http://members.aol.com	com means it is commercial and as there is no country it must be the USA

A C T I V I T Y

a) Which of the above addresses will give the most biased information and why?
b) Which of the above will give the most reliable information and why?
c) Which of the above are academic sites or government or companies?
d) Which address is the odd one out and why?

2 Using Search Engines

The second way to search or look for information is to use key words along with the search engines. A search engine quickly looks at all the addresses in the system and points out the ones with your key words in the address.

Remember you are smarter than the computer so use your intelligence. You may need to use a variety of words, which will mean the same thing.

Choose a search engine from the home page. If you know about a good search engine and you know the address then type the address into the location section and press enter.

A good search engine to try is *www.google.com* It searches very quickly and will locate phrases. Another useful search engine in *www.copernic.com*, which simultaneously consults the best search, engines and provides relevant results with summaries. This search engine takes approximately 45 minutes to download when you use it for the first time.

3 Using Key Words

It is important to use a variety of key words to access information e.g. if you are looking for information about children's toys, the word 'toys' on its' own will bring millions of possible sites. If you enter 'soft toys' then this will narrow the search down. If you enter 'soft, furry toys' then you should get web sites which are much more specific. It is no longer necessary to include 'and', 'not', 'or' if you are using the more recent search engines.

Book marking

Once you have found a good website you should bookmark it. Click on the bookmark or favourite sign and then click on save. The next time you want to look at the site click on 'bookmarks' or 'favourites' and the name of the site will be there, click on it and you will be connected. When the list becomes too long then you can arrange your favourites in folders and alphabetic order.

Printing

When you find a page that you think is going to be useful it is usually possible to print it. A good idea is to go to print preview and see how many pages there are. It will also show you what will actually be printed. It is also useful to highlight the part that you want to print and then press print. Always print on 'draft' or econoprint' to save ink from your cartridge.

Selecting relevant information

Be careful! Anyone can publish on the web. You need to check the validity of your information before using it for assignments.

Here are five techniques to consider:

Authority   Is it clear who is sponsoring the pages? Check the address.

Accuracy   Are there links to outside sources, to verify the information?

Objectivity   Is it clear why the information is there – advertising, information?

Date   Is the information up to date? A good web page is updated regularly.

Coverage   Is the page finished or being written?

Good web pages give the author's name and credentials as well as an indication of when the web site was last updated.

Take care! Many web sites exist to sell information.

ACTIVITY

Copy and complete the table below using the web addresses – some of the columns will be used more than once. The first one has been done for you.

www.uk-legislation.hmso.gov.uk

www.ncb.org.uk

www.niss.ac.uk

www.earlychildhoodnews.com

www.cache.org.uk

www.nspcc.org.uk

www.eb.com

www.monash.com

www.irsc.org

www.childcare-info.co.uk

www.open.gov.uk

www.nichd.nih.gov

www.piaget.org

www.inlandrevenue.co.uk

www.unison.org.uk

www.google.com

www.highscope.org

www.bbc.co.uk

	USA	UK	Full name, where appropriate
Organisation		www.early-education.org.uk	British Association for Early Childhood Education
Appropriate government bodies			
Commercial			
Company			
College			

When you have found each web site, 'bookmark' it and complete the third column. By 'book marking' the sites, you will have a good resource to use when completing assessments.

ACTIVITY

Copy and complete the table below *before* going online and save yourself some time and money!

Topic	Child protection	ADHD	Safety in the home
Possible search words			
Synonyms, other possible search words or phrases			
Checking the • validity • authority • accuracy • objectivity • date • coverage			
Search page address Bookmark			

Recording the source of your information

Once you have found information that will be of use to you, it is essential to make a note of the title, author, date of publication, publisher and page numbers so that you can find the information again at a later date.

ACTIVITY

Match the words to the appropriate definitions below.

Author   Publisher   Content   Index   Preface

1 List at the beginning showing the chapters
2 The writer of the book
3 List at the end showing where the information is in the book
4 Brief overview of the book
5 The company who has printed the book

Remember you can copy information from books, journals or the Internet **only if you say where it has come from** i.e. reference it. Your tutor will very quickly find the work that you have copied word for word because they are very familiar with the text books that they have recommended. Copying without giving credit is called plagiarism and you can lose marks if you do it.

Referencing

When you are writing an assignment it can be helpful to make reference to what you have read in books, journals or information from the Internet. It can help to strengthen your argument or it can show that you have researched the subject area.

Referencing can be done in a number of different ways. Some systems that are used can be extremely complicated and confusing. What is important is that you are consistent in how you use the system chosen by your college or study centre. The methods used below are one way of referencing.

SHORT QUOTATIONS

Quotations that are shorter than 40 words can be written into the text of your assignment. The author's surname and initials are given along with the date of publication and page number(s).

> Young babies need to be cared for by the same adult or a small team of people. O'Hagan states 'If the carers of the baby are constantly changing this will lead to the child feeling insecure'.
>
> (O'Hagan, 1997:84)

Although quotations marks are normally used for shorter quotations they are not used for longer quotations.

LONG QUOTATIONS I.E. 40 WORDS OR MORE

> During pregnancy it is very important for the mother to have a well balanced diet. According to O'Hagan,
>
>> The old wives' saying of 'eating for two' is not true as it is the quality of the food and type of food consumed which is important, not the quantity. During the pregnancy the woman should gain about 12.7kg and 70% of this weight increase should occur during the last 20 weeks of the pregnancy.
>>
>> (O'Hagan 1997:87–88)
>
> It is also important for pregnant women to eat a range of different foods, which contain protein, fats, vitamins, carbohydrate and minerals.

Longer quotations are indented on both sides. They should also have a space between your text and the text that you are going to write after the quotation. This will help to make the quotation stand out.

INDIRECT QUOTATIONS

Sometimes it is not appropriate to write the exact words of a quotation directly from a book or journal but you can still make reference to it in your assignment.

> When planning the early years curriculum for young children it is essential to take account of the children's needs and interests. The Foundation Stage introduced in England in May 2000 reinforces the importance of providing opportunities for children to engage in activities and experiences that are initiated by themselves.
>
> (Curriculum Guidance for the Foundation Stage May 2000)

Creating a bibliography

A bibliography is a list of all the books, journals, newspapers, web sites that you have looked at when preparing your assignment. It should be written at the end of your assignment in alphabetical order by author's surnames. The information that you need to include in the bibliography is usually found in the first few pages of the book or journal.

If you are completing a dissertation or small-scale research your bibliography will contain considerably more detailed information and you should refer to more detailed books on how to create bibliographies. However, for the purposes of most level 2 and level 3 courses the information given below is sufficient.

INFORMATION REQUIRED FOR ALL BOOKS

Surname, initial, year of publication, title of book, place of publication, publisher, in that order.

The date on each entry usually has brackets around it and the title of the book is either underlined or written in italics. If the information takes up more than one line then a 'hanging indent' is used in the second and third line.

Lindon, J. (1998) *Child Protection and Early Years Work* London: Hodder and Stoughton.

ADDITIONAL INFORMATION FOR TWO OR MORE AUTHORS

For two or more authors you need to alter the positioning of the initials for the second and subsequent writers.

Bruce, T. and C. Meggitt (1999) *Child Care and Education.* 2nd Edn. London: Hodder and Stoughton.

IDENTIFYING THAT THE AUTHORS ARE EDITORS

If the authors are editors this shows that the book contains chapters that have been written by a number of different people.

Utting, D. (ed) (1998) *Children's Services Now and in the Future.* London: National Children's Bureau.

WHERE THE TEXT USED IS NOT THE FIRST EDITION

If the book is a second or third edition then you provide the same details as before but include the original published date at the end of the reference. The first date that is written is the most recent date.

Lindon, J. (1997) *Working with Young Children*. London: Hodder and Stoughton (first published 1983).

INFORMATION REQUIRED FOR JOURNALS

If you use journals you should write the information as shown below.

Ollis, J. and E. Nicol (2000) 'What are your training needs?' *Early Education* 30, Spring, 9.

The authors details come first followed by the year of the journal. The title of the article is given and the title of the journal is then underlined. The volume number is included and the page number(s) of the article are then given.

REFERENCING ELECTRONIC SOURCES

Systems for referencing electronic sources are still being developed. The major sources of information regarding electronic sources come from the Internet or CD ROMs. Always try to identify as much information as possible i.e. author/editor, (year), book title (edition) full address details or CD ROM supplier, access date.

Sewell, L. (1999) *Supporting Sure Start Trailblazers*. *www.gingerbread.org.uk/surestar.htlm* (Accessed 2000, May 17)

ACTIVITY

Use the information on this and the following page to create a bibliography.

Orders: please contact Bookpoint Ltd, 78 Milton Park, Abingdon, Oxon OX14 4TD. Telephone: (44) 01235 827720, Fax: (44) 01235 400454. Lines are open from 9.00–6.00, Monday to Saturday, with a 24 hour message answering service. Email address: orders@bookpoint.co.uk

British Library Cataloguing in Publication Data
A catalogue record for this title is available from The British Library

ISBN 0 340 774 568

First published 2000
Impression number   10 9 8 7 6 5 4 3 2 1
Year   2005 2004 2003 2002 2001 2000

Copyright © 2000 Sara Williams and Susan Goodman

Typeset by Fakenham Photosetting Ltd, Fakenham, Norfolk.
Printed in Great Britain for Hodder & Stoughton Educational, a division of Hodder Headline Plc, 338 Euston Road, London NW1 3BH by J.W. Arrowsmith Ltd., Bristol

Reading effectively

It can save a lot of time if you are able to read the information that you have found effectively. The better you understand what you read and remember, the better you will do in your assessments. On way to do this is to use a method called PSQ5R i.e. purpose, survey, question, 5 R's (read, recite, write, reflect, review). There are eight steps to this method.

Step 1   Purpose
Before you start to read the material, ask yourself why you are reading it.

You have to know what you are looking for if the reading is going to be effective.

Step 2   Survey
Briefly look at the information so that you can become familiar with it. Read the headings and subheadings. Get a feel for the main topics.

Step 3   Question
From the headings and sub headings in the reading material, ask yourself some questions about the subject e.g.

What is the reading material about?
What message did the writer intend to get across?
How does the information relate to what I already know?
What experiences have I had that relate to what I am reading?

Step 4   Read
Now read the information slowly and carefully.

Step 5   Recite
Once you have read the information, answer the questions from step 3. This will help you to check how well you have understood the content and will help you to remember what you have read.

Step 6   Write
Write down what you have learned from reading the information. Do not re-write large sections of the material word for word. This is not helpful and wastes time.

Step 7   Review
Go over the material one more time. Concentrate on the questions from step 3 that you found particularly difficult to understand.

Writing effective notes

Did you know that studies have shown that most individuals forget more than 60% of the information that they are given during a class, within 24 hours? Within several days of a class, what you are able to remember will be minimal.

Class time will be where you gain a significant amount of information on the subject you are studying, however if you cannot write effective notes, you will not be able to find the details you want at a later stage.

Before the class begins

1 Read your notes from the previous session.
2 Arrive at your class in time to choose your seat and get organised before the teaching begins. If you are late you will spend the next few minutes trying to catch up.
3 Sit as close to the front of the class as you can. You are less likely to be distracted and you will be able to hear and see clearly.
4 Use a loose-leaf file. This allows you to keep your notes, handouts, photocopies etc. in the correct order.
5 Separate your notes from different classes by using dividers or use a separate file.

At the beginning of the class remember to write:

• The date and title of the unit you are studying
• The title of the class
• The aims and objectives of the session. These are a useful summary.
• The page number of the notes e.g.1/5, 2/5, 3/5 The first number refers to the page and the second number refers to the unit being studied.

When the teaching has started:

1 Listen carefully. Your tutor will use key words that will tell you to pay particular attention to the information given.
2 Use a system for taking notes that is effective and suits you.
3 Write your notes in short sentences and make them as legible as possible. The time spent re-writing notes can be better spent re-reading them and improving your understanding of them.
4 Use abbreviations e.g. chldn, cog dev. However, do not use too many or you may not be able to re-read your notes at a later date.
5 Ask questions if you do not understand the information being given.
6 Do not try to take down everything that your tutor says. It is impossible and unnecessary. Spend more time listening and take down the main points.
7 If you fall behind in your note taking, ask the tutor to repeat the information. You will probably find that others in the group are having the same problem.

8 Avoid underlining and highlighting your notes to make them look attractive, particularly during group discussions or other occasions when you are not writing notes. You may miss important information and it also wastes valuable time. Remember you are the only person who is going to read them.

After the class

1 Re-read your notes as soon as possible as it will help you to review the information that you have been given.
2 Ask your tutor to explain sections you have not understood. Often you find that it is not until you re-read your notes that the information is confusing.
3 Compare your notes with a friend. You may find that they have written information that you have missed and vice versa.

Key words to listen for during the class

If you hear any of these phrases during your class, listen carefully because the information that will follow will often clarify or summarise what you have just heard.

The three main reasons	Listen for three points that are going to be made
On the other hand	This tells you that a different point of view is going to be considered
For example	A tutor will often try to provide a practical example to help to explain a point. This can be extremely valuable.
In other words	Your tutor is going to explain a point in a simple way.
In conclusion	Listen carefully as your tutor is going to summarise what has been taught during the session. Take detailed notes as it will be useful for revision.

The Cornell Note-taking System

The Cornell note-taking system makes it easier to highlight and remember the main ideas of the class or information from the text book.

Step 1   Prepare your note paper before you begin to write your notes

Divide your note paper into two sections by drawing a line down the page with ¼ to the left of the line and ¾ to the right. The right hand column is used for writing your notes during the class while the left hand column is used after the session to highlight the main ideas of the text and any key words or technical words that are appropriate.

¼ of the page Main ideas Key words Technical words	¾ of the page Detailed notes taken during class/from text At the bottom of the last page of notes leave a space for a summary of the class.

When you begin to revise for examinations you can cover up the right hand side of your page and use the left hand side to see how much you can remember.

ACTIVITY

Read the notes that a student has started to make on the Foundation Stage. Complete the left hand column by identifying the main points and any key/technical words. How could the student have made the notes easier to re-read?

	Unit Title *Working with Young Children* The Foundation Stage and the Areas of Learning 6 May 2000 Aim 1 To define the term 'Foundation Stage' 2 To identify the different areas of learning 3 To plan activities or experiences for each area of learning

The Foundation Stage
This stage is for children from 3 years to the end of reception year. They will be introduced in September 2000 in nursery schools or classes, playgroups, day nurseries and childminders who receive funding from the government. The children will be assessed according to the early learning goals. Stepping stones have been identified which show how the children progress from one stage to another.

Areas of Learning
There are six areas of learning.
Communication, language and literacy
Mathematical development
Personal, social and emotional development
Physical development
Creative development
Knowledge and understanding of the world

Step 2   Action replay

As soon as possible after the class, try to summarise the main points that were raised. This does not have to be written down, you could do it in your head. If you cannot do it, read through your notes and try again. If you still cannot do it, then it may be sensible to go back to your tutor for extra help as you may not have fully understood the subject that was being discussed.

Step 3   Talk to yourself

Did you know that students who recite facts or main ideas out loud,
remember information much better than those who just re-read the same
information to themselves. So, why not try it? Say each fact out loud as it
can help you to remember. You could do it while you are having a bath,
washing the dishes, listening to music . . .

Step 4   Think back

Go back to your notes and spend time thinking through the information.
What are the main ideas, what technical terms are important and can you
define them in your own words, how does the information relate to what
you know already?

Step 5   Time and time again

Re-read your notes at every opportunity particularly if you have an
examination on the subject area. It is much easier to learn the information
over a period of time than cramming at the last minute.

3

Writing Assignments

The aim of this chapter is to help you

- understand the purpose of assignments
- identify key words that tell you what to do
- read and understand the assignment
- write assignments
- understand the marking/grading criteria.

The purpose of assignments

The purpose of an assignment is to test your knowledge and understanding of the subject that you are studying, your ability to apply your knowledge to a practical situation and your ability to evaluate and analyse the subject.

When you write your assignment you will also be able to demonstrate:

- how well you can research a topic;
- your ability to gather relevant information;
- your ability to write in an appropriate format.

Most qualifications will use assignments as one of the methods of assessment. Other assessments may include multiple choice question papers, short answer papers, examinations or research projects e.g. if you are working towards the Diploma in Child Care and Education you will be required to complete unit assignments, a portfolio for Unit 1 'Observation and Assessment', a portfolio for Unit 2 'Work with Young Children' and an examination at the end of the course.

Advantages and disadvantages of writing an assignment

Advantages	Disadvantages
The work can be completed at home and in your own time	You may spend a lot of time trying to find information, only to find that you cannot use it because it is not appropriate.
The task can be completed over a number of weeks	You need to have good time management skills or you may find that you do not leave yourself enough time to complete the work
You can discuss the assignment with other students and your tutor (however you must remember that the work you submit is all your own work and not another students)	You can spend a lot of time writing, re-writing and then re-writing your work and it does not guarantee that you have a better assignment at the end.

Different methods of writing an assignment

You may be asked to write your assignment in a number of different ways. These include:

Report

A report is a way of giving information and recommendations about a particular topic. If you are writing a report you will have carried out an investigation into the topic. The investigation will be the information you have gathered to answer the various tasks. Sometimes you will find the information by looking it up or by asking people questions.

A report has a structure, i.e.:
- introduction
- procedure/method
- findings
- conclusion
- recommendation.

Case study

A case study is a description of a situation. You may be asked to write a case study when you are in the work setting or you may be given a case study as part of your assignment. You will be asked questions based on the information that you are given in the case study.

Leaflet

This is a relatively short piece of work as you are usually only required to write on an A4 sheet of paper however it does mean that you need to be very concise when providing information. Bullet points, charts, tables and illustrations may be used to provide the information.

Brochure/booklet

This is usually a number of A4 pages folded to A5 and stapled in the middle. Once again bullet points, tables etc. would be used to provide the information. Descriptive paragraphs would not be expected.

Chart

Information is normally provided on A3 sized paper. A title is given and bullet points, illustrations etc are used.

Essay

This is a more formal style of assignment. The structure of the essay would normally include:

- an introduction
- the main text, which is usually divided into paragraphs
- conclusion
- references and bibliography.

When assignments are written, key words are included to assess:

- your knowledge and understanding;
  your ability to interpret and apply;
  your ability to evaluate the information.

Knowledge and understanding	Interpretation and application	Evaluation
Outline	Identify	Assess
Explain	Illustrate	Evaluate
Examine	Using	To what extent . . .?
Describe	Give an example	How useful. . . ?
State	Suggest	Critically discuss
Name	How might . . .?	Compare and contrast

It is important that you understand what they mean.

Key words that tell you what to do

- **account for**   explain and go into detail about the main points
- **compare**   look for and explain the points which are the same, and the points which are different
- **contrast**   highlight the differences
- **define**   give the precise meaning of the word, phrase or topic
- **discuss**   examine the topic through arguments for and against, write as if it was a debate
- **describe**   give a detailed account
- **differentiate/distinguish**   look for and highlight the differences

- **evaluate**   make an appraisal, show the value of
- **explain**   make plain, interpret the meaning of
- **interpret**   make clear what the topic is about
- **illustrate**   make clear what the topic is about by
                             giving examples
- **justify**   give reasons for the decision/conclusion
- **outline**   give the main features/general principles
- **state**   give the information in a brief
                             uncomplicated form
- **summarise**   make a precise account of the main points
                             leaving out the detail and the examples

Who is the assignment being written for?

Before you begin to write the assignment it is important to know who the task is aimed at, as it will influence how you write your assignment.

Parents/students
- More personal language may be used e.g. 'you'
- Illustrations, charts and tables may be included
- Technical terms may need to be explained

Professional workers e.g. social workers, teachers, medical profession
- Formal language should be used i.e. do not use 'I' or 'you'
- It may be assumed that the majority of technical terms are understood
- Illustrations should only be used if they are explaining a specific issue e.g. areas on the body where a child has been abused
- Charts, tables and graphs may be used to reinforce significant facts

No audience is given
- Formal language should be used i.e. do not use 'I' or 'you'
- Graphs, tables, charts may be used

Assignment guidelines

The guidelines for an assignment will vary from one awarding body to another however, they will all contain similar information.

It is very important to read the whole assignment through, as each section will contain useful information.

Assignments may have different sections e.g.

1 An outline of the assignment task

This section will give you details about the assignment. Information will include:

- what you are going to do
- who the intended audience will be
- how you should present your work.

It may also tell you how long your completed work should be and any other information that should be included.

2 Guidance on what you should do before starting the assignment

Detailed information is given in this section on what you may do to prepare for the assignment. It is very important to read this through carefully. You will also find that you will go back to it several times when you are writing the assignment.

3 The knowledge and understanding of the subject that you need to have before beginning the assignment

Before you begin your assignment it is important that you have a good understanding of the subject area. This section will help you to identify the areas that you feel confident in and the areas where you will need to do more research.

4 Grading criteria

This is the final section of your assignment and you may feel that you do not need to read it until after you have completed your work. This is not a good idea. It is very important to read this section carefully BEFORE your begin to plan and write your assignment as it contains vital and possibly additional information which must be included in the completed work.

Writing the assignment

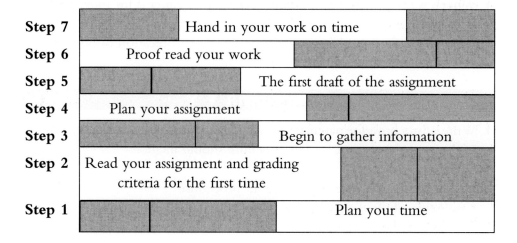

Step 7	Hand in your work on time
Step 6	Proof read your work
Step 5	The first draft of the assignment
Step 4	Plan your assignment
Step 3	Begin to gather information
Step 2	Read your assignment and grading criteria for the first time
Step 1	Plan your time

Step 1 Plan your time

When you receive your assignment you should:

- Write the submission date in your diary or on your wall planner.
- Prepare a time plan for your work. If you miss the submission date you could lose marks, receive a lower grade or fail the assignment.
- Make a note of any assignment workshops or tutorial times that your tutor has organised. Do not miss these dates, as your tutor will provide guidance on how to complete your task.

Step 2 Read your assignment for the first time

Don't panic!

When you receive your assignment for the first time it can be daunting. There is often a lot to read and you may not feel confident about the subject area.

Remember You will have more teaching on the subject area before you have to submit your assignment so do not worry if you do not fully understand the task at the beginning.

Before you start to prepare for your assignment, ask yourself FIVE questions:

1 **Which** assignment method do I have to use e.g. report writing, essay, booklet?
2 **Who** is the assignment aimed at e.g. parents, students?
3 **What** information MUST be included in the assignment in order to gain a pass?
4 **Where** will I get the information? (Refer to Chapter 2 for more detailed information.)
5 **How** much do I need to write e.g. is there any indication of how long the assignment should be?

A C T I V I T Y

1 Write a brochure for parents, which explain the 'settling in' procedures of the pre-school nursery. The brochure should include:

  • a definition of the term 'settling in' procedure
  • an explanation as to why a 'settling in' procedure is important for the child and the parent
  • a description of FIVE different activities/experiences that form part of the 'settling in' procedure.

2 When you have completed your brochure, give it to two different parents who have children in a pre-school nursery and ask them to read it. Ask them for their comments and write a report on the effectiveness of your work.

Read the assignment above and answer the questions below.

  a) Which assignment method(s) do you have to use?
  b) Who is the assignment aimed at?
  c) What information must be included in the assignment?
  d) Where will you get information from to answer the assignment? Try to list as many sources as possible.
  e) How long should the assignment be? If no indication has been given, how will you balance your work i.e. which task will contain more detailed information?

When you have finished, discuss your answers with a colleague.

Having gathered this information, it is important to look at more specific details e.g.:

- How many tasks and/or questions do you need to complete?
- How many marks have been allocated to each task? The greater the number of marks, the more in-depth the answer should be. If no marks are given, it is very important to read the grading criteria.
- Does the assignment relate to a specific age group and/or work setting? If it does, then it is important to base your answer around this information.
- Have any words been highlighted e.g. some words may be written in CAPITAL letters or they may be underlined or written in **bold.** If they are, you should pay particular attention to them as the assignment writer feels that they are very important and want to draw your attention to them.

Step 3 Find information and make notes

Collect the information gradually and be prepared to change your plans in the light of what you read. However, it is very important that you do not leave things to the last minute.

It is very important when gathering information for an assignment to make detailed notes that can be easily referred to when you begin to write your assignment.

MAKING NOTES

Possible resources for the assignment 'Settling in Procedures' could include:

- The settling in procedures from a variety of different nurseries (If you use any of this material in your work, it is important to receive permission from the nursery and to maintain confidentiality.)
- College notes
- Notes from your placement. These may be written as a result of interviewing members of staff and/or parents.
- Nursery World magazine
- Relevant text books including 'Child Care and Education' by Tina Bruce and Carolyn Meggit 1999
- Child care organisations e.g. Early Education, National Children's Bureau, Pre-school Learning Alliance, National Childminding Association

Helpful hint Always compile your references and bibliography section as you work your way through the assignment. It avoids doing a very boring job when you have finished and can save time.

Step 4 Plan your assignment

You will never be able to gather sufficient information for your assignment so there will come a time when you have to stop researching and begin to write. Before you begin writing, it can be useful to plan what you are going to do. It can be useful to draw a mind map to show the main areas that you want to include.

A C T I V I T Y

Using the assignment entitled 'Settling in Procedures' make a rough plan of how you would develop your assignment. The main headings could be the format shown above. It may be useful to brainstorm your ideas with a friend.

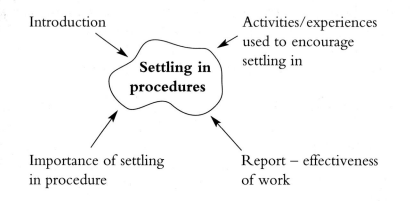

Step 5 The first draft of your assignment

The hardest part of any assignment is getting started so it can useful to begin with a section that you understand and have confidence to write about. However, always remember to keep referring back to the assignment, as it can be very easy to miss out sections or include information that is not relevant. Always remember that the marker will be looking for quality information and not necessarily quantity.

a) Begin by brainstorming the topic and write down <u>all</u> your ideas that you have gained from your information search on the subject. You will sift out some of these ideas at a later stage but write them all down at this stage. Go through your list and think about each one. Decide what to use and what to leave out.

b) Before you start to write, organise your ideas. Write an outline to the answer. This could be notes, bullet points or a list. Put your ideas in order of priority. This will help to form paragraphs at a later stage.

c) Organise your answer i.e. tell the reader what the subject is about, give them detailed information about the subject and summarise what you have told the reader.

The answer may be in three sections:

Introduction – This is where you introduce the subject. State clearly the points that you are going to make in the assessment. It explains to the reader why you are writing the paper.

The main body of the text – This section may consist of one or more paragraphs. The first sentence should tell the reader about the subject of the paragraph. The following sentences will give detailed information. The last sentence should lead the reader into the next paragraph.

The conclusion – This is the section where you sum up your ideas. Do not be tempted to rush this section as it is very important. Make sure that the introduction agrees with the conclusion i.e. make sure that you have done what you said you would do in the introduction. You may also add any insights or final thoughts you have on the topic in the conclusion.

Certain words can help to show that you understand the subject area.

Interpretation	Application
The relevance of this	Illustrated by
This indicates	Support for this
This is similar to / different from	As shown by
So	This can be seen in
Therefore	For example
This means / does not mean	This can be applied to
A consequence of	This is associated with
The implication of	This leads to
The contrast between	This touches on
Put simply	The same applies to
	This is confirmed by

Adapted from Moores (1999) *Do you have a skills deficit in essay writing?* Sociology Review January 1999:22–23

Designing brochures or leaflets

If you are designing a brochure or information leaflet it is important to arrange the information in an appropriate way.

A C T I V I T Y

This activity could be completed by yourself or with a colleague. (Do not write a detailed content for the brochure. The purpose of the activity is to help you design a suitable format for a brochure.)

- Decide which size of paper you are going to use e.g. A4 full size or A4 folded to A5.
- Estimate how many pages you are going to need. You may need to re-think this when you start to put in the information. If a word limit has been given, this will need to be considered when deciding on the number of pages that you are going to use.
- Decide the order that you are going to put the information in to.
- Choose a suitable title and decide where you are going to place it in your brochure.
- Choose subtitles for each section.
- Make a draft copy of the brochure. This should include the subtitles, sufficient space for the written information you want to include and space for any illustrations, charts etc you would like to use.

1 What difficulties did you encounter?
2 What advantages would be gained by word processing the brochure rather than handwriting it?

Step 6 Proof read your work and add or amend if necessary

This is a very important task and should not be missed out no matter how short of time you are before the submission date. Always remember to re-read and spell-check your work to ensure that there are no obvious errors in the text.

Helpful hint It can be useful to ask someone else to proof read your work, as they will spot errors that you have missed.

Step 7 Presenting your assignment

It is very important to take time to present your work in a professional way. Marks or a higher grade may be awarded for presentation in some assignments.

Basic writing skills

Write complete sentences

A complete sentence is a sentence you can say to someone, and the person will understand it. You have included a subject and a verb.

Use correct punctuation

- Sentences end with a full stop.
- Questions end with a question mark.
- Use exclamation marks for exclamations and commands.
- Commas tell the reader to pause.
- Avoid making your sentences too long and complex.

Be clear and brief

- Say what you mean.
- Think about the words you are going to use.
- Stick to the subject.
- Keep your reader interested.

Write in a natural style

- Writing, like a conversation, should flow naturally.
- Only use technical words if you understand them and can use them accurately.
- Make sure that the reader understands your ideas.
- Read your finished assignment to a friend to see if they understand what you are trying to say.

Some more helpful hints

- Remember to put your name on each page of the assignment.
- Make sure your work is legible. Most awarding bodies will expect you to word process your work but if you are hand writing the assignment always make sure the reader can read it.
- Guide the reader find their way through your assignment. Use titles, sub headings and bullet points.
- Answer every section of the assignment. Check the grading criteria to make sure you have not missed anything out.

Advantages of word processing assignments

Advantages	Disadvantages
• It is easy to read.	• It can be time consuming if you are not familiar with the key board or software programmes.
• Information within the text can be moved around easily.	• Accessing equipment may be difficult if you do not have your own.
• Space can be left for illustrations, charts etc.	• The work must be proof read carefully because the spell-check will not identify words with the same sounds but different meanings e.g. their/there
• A scanner may be used to import images, illustrations etc.	
• A spell-check may be used to ensure accurate spelling.	
• The final presentation of the work can look very professional.	

Ten simple checks to make before you submit your work for assessment.

Assignment checklist

Tick when it has been checked

1   Personal details are written on each piece of paper that has been used i.e. name, registration number, study centre details. This information may be inserted in the header or footer if you are word processing your assignment.

2   Awarding body information has been attached and completed e.g. assignment task.

3   The number of words used on the assignment has been indicated, if required. The word processor can do this for you automatically. Click on 'tools' and then on 'word count'.

4   Page numbers have been inserted. It can also be useful for your own reference to include the date. The word processor can do this for you automatically.

5   The work is legible. Ask a friend to give you their opinion.

    A suitable print size and font have been used if word-processed. Print size 12 or 14 are often used.

6   The work has been proof read for the correct use of spelling, grammar and punctuation.

7   All the questions/sections have been answered.

8   Check the grading criteria to make sure that all the information has been included.

9   A reference and bibliography section has been included.

10 The work has been collated in a professional way e.g. stapled, bound. The collation of your final work will depend on the number of pages that you have used. Discuss with your tutor if it is appropriate to use clear pockets.

Spell-check

Although it is possible to use spell-checks on a computer, an early years worker must be able to spell accurately in order to help the children's spelling skills. It can be useful to have rules, phrases or mnemonics as reminders e.g. ' i before e except after c'. There are always exceptions to the rule but it can make spelling an easier task. The list below gives some examples of the common words that are used by early years students and suggestions on how to spell them accurately.

Hints to help you	
accommodation	Two **c**ots and two **m**attresses!
beautiful	**b**oys **e**at apples **u**nder **tr**ees **in** France **un**til **l**unch
dessert	**s**weet and **st**icky
great	it's g**reat** to **eat**
intelligent	**tell** the **gent** to come in
parallel	parallel has three lines
se*para*te	Never separate a para from his parachute
Tuesday	**u e**at **s**weets day
Wednesday	**n**ever **e**at **s**weets day
Thursday	This is the **u r** sick day

Other helpful hints
there, their and they're If there can be a 'my' spell 'their' with an 'i'. You can say 'My house is big'. You can say 'Their house is big'. You can't say 'He lives my'. But you can say 'He lives there'. You can't say 'My in the garden'. You can say 'They're in the garden'.
past – passed Passed is a verb – a doing word. Mary passed her driving test. In the past we lived in France.
to – two – too I go to school. We have two cars. He is too tired.

ACTIVITY

Use an address book and create a spelling book of the most common words that you use during your course. It could include words such as cognitive, development, practice, environment etc. It may also help to write the meaning of the word along side it. Your spelling book could then become a useful resource when you revise for examinations.

You're late!

If you think you are not going to complete your assignment on time it is very important to talk to your tutor as soon as possible. He/she may be able to give you a few extra days before handing in your completed work but you may only achieve a pass for your work. Different awarding bodies have different procedures for late submission, so it is very important that you know the rules before you begin working on your assignment.

Making your assignment better

It is always difficult when you receive a refer because you are bound to feel upset and the thought of doing more work on the assignment will not be a pleasant one.

However, it is very important that you:

1 arrange a tutorial with the subject tutor as soon as possible, to ask where you have missed out information or not given sufficient information.
2 take notes at the meeting or you will forget what was said when you begin to work on your assignment.
3 begin work on the assignment as soon as possible because you will have a new hand in date and you will be starting new subjects which will also have an assessment.
4 talk to your tutor if you do not feel confident about specific areas.
5 take your tutor's advice, provide the additional information and submit the work on time, or before if possible.

You may be given the opportunity to upgrade your work from a pass or merit to a higher grade however, it is very important to take the following factors into consideration:

a) Do you have time to write a new assignment?

b) Could re-writing your assignment jeopardise the grade you receive for your next assignment?

c) How close to the next grade were you? If you were very close it might be worth attempting to up grade your work.

Before you make a final decision, take time to think through *all* the implications, talk to friends or your family AND discuss it with your tutor.

4

Preparing for examinations

> ## *The aim of this chapter is to help you*
>
> - understand the different types of examinations you may have to complete
> - answer different types of questions
> - find different ways of revising for examinations.

All awarding bodies are required to assess students through external assessments. Different awarding bodies use different assessment methods. To achieve some qualifications you must pass a variety of assessments. Assignments have already been considered in Chapter 3.

Short answer papers, extended answer papers and multiple choice question papers are completed at your study centre on specific dates. You may not be allowed to use textbooks, notes or other resources. You have to remember the information that you have been taught and answer the questions on the paper. This demands different skills and preparation to that of writing assignments.

Short answer papers

A short answer paper is made up of a set number of questions which must be answered within a specific time, usually between one or two hours. Most awarding bodies give you a question book, which you write the answers in. If you need more space, then you need to ask for more paper. Always remember to write the question number and your name on any additional paper you use.

The questions are written in a variety of different formats.

Simple statements

The example below shows that the question can be a simple statement. Can you answer it?

List THREE signs or symptoms of mumps.

....

....

....

3 marks

When answering this type of short answer question remember to:

- read the question carefully
- look for any key words e.g. list, name, describe, explain. This will give you a clue as to how much you have to write.
- look for any words that are in **bold**, CAPITAL letters, <u>underlined</u> as these show that they are important to the question
- look at the number of marks that have been allocated. This tells you how many facts you must give in order to gain all the marks.

Your answers for the short answer question may have included the following answers:

- swelling of jaw in front of ears
- fever
- sore to eat and drink
- swollen face.

The question asked you to LIST so it is not necessary to write long descriptions for the answer. This will take time, which you could use to answer longer questions.

The word THREE has been written in capital letters. This tells you that you <u>must</u> give three answers. If you give two very detailed answers you will only be allocated two marks.

Three marks have been allocated to the question. This also tells you that you do not need to write long descriptions.

Descriptions

The marker would expect you to write in sentences when answering this question. It can be useful to highlight the words that you need to focus on e.g. describe, physical play.

> Briefly describe the term 'physical development'.
>
> ....
>
> ....
>
> ....
>
> 4 marks

If you were answering this question, you would write four different facts. The description could include information about:

- development of use of muscles etc.
- gross motor skills e.g. football
- fine manipulative skills e.g. using scissors
- hand and eye co-ordination e.g. threading beads.

Examples could also be included to support your answer.

Questions containing more detailed information

If a question contains more detailed information it is very important to take account of the details. Highlighting the key words is extremely useful in this type of question. Three marks would be awarded for information given on 'during the tantrum' and three marks would be awarded for information given on 'after the tantrum'.

> How can the adult help a two year old child who is having a temper tantrum? Explain what he/she would do during AND after the tantrum.
>
> ....
>
> ....
>
> ....
>
> ....
>
> 6 marks

Charts, tables and illustrations

Charts, tables or illustrations may be used for short answer papers. They can be a bit daunting when you look at them for the first time. However it is important to remember, that they are assessing your knowledge of a subject that you have revised for.

Before you read the questions, look at the following information:

- The title of the chart as this will give you a clear indication of the subject that is being considered.
- The axis titles as this will give you more specific information.
- The dates of the survey or when the statistics were collated. This can give you some useful information e.g. if the survey was carried out in the 1970s the circumstances that affected low income households would be very different from the 1990s.
- The source of the information.
- The pattern of the graph. In the example below you can see that the United States has a high percentage of children in low-income households and Finland has a low percentage of children in low-income households.

When you have completed these simple steps, you will have gained a considerable amount of information. This will build up your confidence and allow you to answer the questions more effectively.

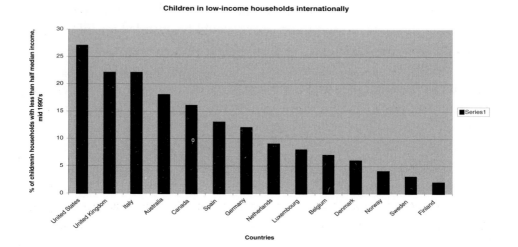

Source Bradbury, B and Jantti, M (1999) *Child Poverty Across the Industrialised Nations,* UNICEF International Child Development Centre, Innocenti Occasional paper, Economic and Social Policy series no. 71

1 Which country has the lowest percentage of children in low income households? **1 mark**

2 Briefly describe the United Kingdom's position in relation to other international countries with regard to children in low income households. **4 marks**

3 Describe the effects that poverty can have on young children and their families? **5 marks**

The last question expects you to use your own knowledge of poverty. Reference would not be made to the graph unless it was relevant.

ACTIVITY

Read the question below.

How can the early years worker prepare a three year old child for a planned admission to hospital? Describe THREE activities/experiences that may be used in the pre-school nursery.

9 marks

Now read the answer that was given by the student.

The early years worker could change the home area into a hospital area. Doctor and nurse uniforms could be laid out and different pieces of hospital equipment could be given e.g. stethoscope, injections. If the adult was invited into the hospital area he/she could encourage the children to talk about the situation.

The early years worker could explain to the child what will happen and ask the child to write a diary of his/her experiences when they are in the hospital.

You have been asked to mark this work. How many marks would you give and what advice would you give to the student to improve his/her marks?

Now read what the tutor wrote as comments:
Activity 1 – Well done. This would be a very suitable activity for the child. You have included examples of resources and shown the role of the adult in promoting the experience.   *3 marks*

Activity 2 – A brief explanation has been given as to how the adult would help the child understand this experience however the activity is inappropriate as it is unlikely that the child could write a diary. A more appropriate activity would be to encourage the child to draw a picture.   *1 mark*

Activity 3 – Unfortunately this activity/experience has not been given.   *0 marks*

Total 4 marks out of a possible 9

A C T I V I T Y

Answer the questions below. (If you are using these questions as a practice for your short answer papers, you should allow yourself forty five minutes to complete the paper.) The awarding body that you are using may not have short answer papers. You could use these questions for revision purposes.

1 List THREE signs or symptoms of chicken pox.

3 marks

2 A child is going to be in hospital for a number of weeks. Describe TWO ways in which the early years worker can support the child during his/her stay in hospital.

4 marks

3 Give TWO examples of professional workers who can support a family with a child who has sickle cell anaemia.

2 marks

4 Describe how the nanny would care for a three year old child who has a heavy cold in the home.

8 marks

5 How should medicines be stored in the home?

3 marks

6 List FOUR common triggers of asthma.

4 marks

7 How can the early years worker care for a child experiencing an asthma attack in school? Describe THREE different actions.

6 marks

8 a) List THREE signs or symptoms that would indicate that a child is not well.

3 marks

    b) Give TWO examples of signs or symptoms that a child with different skin tones is not well.

2 marks

9 Give THREE reasons why children are immunised.

3 marks

10 Name TWO professionals who may work as part of the primary health care team.

2 marks

Total 40 marks   Pass grade 20 marks   Merit grade 26 marks
Distinction grade 32 marks
How well did you do?

ACTIVITY

Write some short answer questions yourself and ask a friend on your course to answer them. (Make sure you know the answers before giving them to your friend!) They can write some questions too and ask you to answer them.

All you need to do is:

- look at the syllabus for the unit that is to be tested
- choose one of the learning objectives
- decide whether or not to make it an easy or a difficult question
- use the key words that you have already seen in the sample papers e.g. list, describe, name

- allocate marks
- give them to your friend.

It is fun and a good way to revise.

This short answer paper is based on health and safety issues, food and nutrition and the care of young children.

A C T I V I T Y

Answer the questions below. (If you are using these questions as a practice for your short answer papers, you should allow yourself forty five minutes to complete the paper.)

1 Describe THREE examples of promoting positive gender images in a nursery for three to five year old children.

6 marks

2 How can the nanny ensure that the kitchen is safe and hygienic? List SIX different examples.

6 marks

3 Explain why it is important that work settings have policies for the safe handling of body fluids.

4 marks

4 List FIVE safety issues that must be taken into account when planning an outing for 5 to 6 year olds.

5 marks

5 Name the nutrients that are essential for a healthy body.

6 marks

6 a) List FIVE potential hazards in the outdoor play area of a nursery.

5 marks

   b) Describe how the early years worker can prevent accidents happening in the outdoor play area.

8 marks

7 Describe TWO ways in which food can be made appealing to young children.

4 marks

8 Explain how the following foods should be stored in the refrigerator. Give reasons for your answers.
   a) raw chicken
   b) cooked meat
   c) raw vegetables

6 marks

9 A four year old child has an allergy to nuts. What precautions can be taken to ensure that the child does not eat nuts in the day nursery?

6 marks

10 Explain why it is important to have a routine for 'home time'.

4 marks

Total	40 marks
Pass	20 marks
Merit	26 marks
Distinction	32 marks

How well did you do?

ACTIVITY

This short answer paper is based on child development.

Answer the questions below. (If you are using these questions as a practice for your short answer papers, you should allow yourself forty-five minutes to complete the paper.)

1 Describe TWO creative activities, which could help a four year old child express his/her feelings. Give reasons for your choice.

4 marks

2 List TWO ways in which the Nursery Nurse can encourage positive images of people with disabilities.

2 marks

3 Name THREE theorists who have studied child development.

3 marks

4 Describe THREE activities, which will promote the gross motor skills of a five year old child. Give reasons for your answer.

6 marks

5 Name THREE toys that could promote the cognitive development of a three year old child.

3 marks

6 Describe how the early years worker can promote the social development of a four year old child who is very shy?

4 marks

7 A two year old child has a temper tantrum in the supermarket.
a)   What may have caused this behaviour?

4 marks

b)   How should the nanny manage the situation?

4 marks

8 Briefly describe the main stages of language development of a child from birth to one year old.

6 marks

9 Describe the meaning of:
a)   solitary play
b)   parallel play

2 marks

10 Name TWO activities that would promote the social development of a seven year old child.

2 marks

Total	40 marks
Pass	20 marks
Merit	26 marks
Distinction	32 marks

How well did you do?

Preparing for the short answer paper

- Make a list of the technical words or phrases that you have used during your course.
- Write down a definition of each term.
- Think of examples or practical illustrations for each word or phrase.
- Work out how the word or phrase is relevant to the unit.

Multiple Choice Question Papers (MCQ)

A multiple choice question has three sections to it:

- the stem
- the key
- three distracters.

The normal temperature taken under the tongue is
This is the stem of the question.

A	35°C	The key is the correct answer and
B	36°C	the distracters are the wrong
C	37°C	answers.
D	38°C	

Which answer is the correct answer? You always give the letter in an MCQ paper rather than the answer itself. In this case the answer would be C.

Each question paper will have a variety of different types of questions, some of which are shown in the examples below.

ACTIVITY

Multiple choice question paper

1 Childminders work in
a) their own home
b) a day nursery
c) a school
d) someone else's home

2 Under the Children Act child-minders must register with the
a) education department
b) social services
c) police
d) health department

3 Parallel play is when a child
a) plays alone but near other children
b) plays alongside another child but does not interact
c) plays alongside another child and interacts
d) plays with another child using the same equipment

4 The Foundation Stage is for children aged between
a) 3 and the end of nursery
b) 3 and the end of reception
c) 3 and the end of year 1
d) 3 and the end of year 2

5 How many areas of learning are there in the Foundation Stage?
a) 5
b) 6
c) 7
d) 8

6 A child has bruises on both arms in exactly the same place. What form of abuse could this indicate?
a) sexual abuse
b) physical abuse
c) neglect
d) emotional abuse

Recording your MCQ answers

The awarding body will provide you with a question booklet and an answer sheet to record your answers on.

The instruction sheet below is used by QCA for external assessment for Key Skills Level 1 Communication.

LEVEL	PAPER
Key Skills – Level 1	Communication

WHAT YOU NEED: (TOTAL MARKS 40)   THERE ARE 40 QUESTIONS IN THIS PAPER
- this question booklet
- an answer sheet
- an HB pencil
- an eraser

ADDITIONAL AIDS
- dictionaries may not be used
- bilingual dictionaries may be used

TIME ALLOWED – 1 HOUR

To complete this activity successfully you will need to:

- read the information supplied in the question booklet;
- use an HB pencil to complete all parts of the answer sheet.

Instructions to candidates
Write your personal details in the spaces provided on the answer sheet.
Do not open this question booklet until you are told to do so by the supervisor.
Read each question carefully and attempt all questions.
At the end of the assessment hand your question booklet, your answer sheet and all notes to your supervisor.

It is very important to read the instructions on the answer sheet before you begin the questions e.g.

- You must NOT record your answers on the question paper. The answer sheets are marked electronically and your answer sheet will have no marks on it therefore you will automatically fail the MCQ.
- You must use a black pencil. The electronic equipment will not accept papers unless a black pencil has been used.
- It is very important to put a mark against every question, even if you are not sure if the answer is correct. No mark = no mark!

Preparing for an MCQ

- Study the facts and the concepts.

- Look through your notes and text books for information that could be answered through an MCQ.
- If past copies of the papers are available, look at the style of the questions available.
- Some text books have MCQ's at the end of each chapter. A useful book is *Introduction to Child Care and Education*, by Meggitt, Stevens and Bruce, 2000 (see Bibliography).

Case studies and scenarios

Case studies and scenarios are often used in examinations. The questions that you have to answer must refer back to the information given in the case study.

A C T I V I T Y

Read the case study and answer the questions. You may find it helpful to highlight key words or phrases.

Jo works as a Key Worker with the four year old children in a day nursery. First thing on Monday morning Peter arrived at the nursery, rushed up to Jo and told her that he had visited the London Eye on Saturday. He was very excited as he described what he had done. He explained that he had gone to London with his dad on a train and then they had taken the underground to Westminster. When they arrived at the London Eye they had to queue for a long time before they could go into the pod. The wheel moved very slowly and Peter said that he saw Big Ben and the Houses of Parliament. He had been a little scared when he looked down at his feet because he could see through the floor. When he got back to the ground his dad bought him a post card of the London Eye.

1 What was Jo's role throughout the conversation with Peter?

3 marks

2 Explain the meaning of the term 'Foundation Stage' as part of the early years curriculum. Name the six areas of learning.

4 marks

3 Draw a detailed chart of the possible activities/experiences that Jo could provide for Peter to develop his interest in the trip. Each area of learning should be included in the chart.

10 marks

4 In the Curriculum Guidance for the Foundation Stage, 'stepping stones' are identified for each area of learning. Describe what is meant by the term 'stepping stones'.

3 marks

5 How can Jo involve the parent in helping Peter to develop his learning as a result of his experience on the London Eye?

5 marks
Total 25 marks

Preparing for case studies and scenarios

- Study the concepts and examples as well as the facts. Remember you need to apply your knowledge to the situation.
- Look at past papers to find out what style the questions is.
- Have a practise run within the time limit laid down by the awarding body.

Improving your memory

Whichever examination you are preparing for, you will need to remember a lot of information. Here are some ideas for improving your memory.

- Repeat and repeat – Say it out loud over and over again or look at it over and over again.
- Use your imagination – create a mental picture of the information that you want to remember e.g. you could relate different types of play to children that you know who have played in that way.
- Draw a diagram or mind map on paper, which summarises the main facts that you want to remember.
- Be silly – create a rap or a poem about the information.
- Use acronyms – most early years students use PIES, PILES or SPLICE to remember the different areas of development.
- Tape it – if you are an auditory learner you may find it easier to put the facts on tape and replay it as often as necessary. Take care that you do not switch off!
- Imagine a path – If you are trying to remember processes or procedures it can help if you visualise them as a path and follow each step through e.g. learning the process of sterilizing bottles.

Remember, if you understand the information you are more likely to be able to remember it.

Exam Revision

Begin your revision for your examinations the day you *start* your course. You can do this by:

- writing good, clear notes;
- completing the homework that your tutor has asked you to do;
- asking questions if you do not understand the subject;
- summarising your notes. You could use index cards, mind maps, tape recordings etc. Whatever you create make it small enough to carry around with you so that you can revise on the train or bus to college, standing in a queue, study periods etc.

Working with a revision group

A revision group is usually when a group of friends meet together to revise. This can be very effective or disastrous. To be effective you need to:

- work with a manageable group size. If there are too many people involved in the revision group it will not be effective;
- work with people who have similar goals to yourself;
- choose a good time and place to meet to revise;
- list your long term goals and make a plan which ensures that you are going to achieve them;
- include breaks in your plan but remember that these can be time wasters;
- set targets for each session but remember to make them realistic keep to your plan;
- avoid distractions. It is very easy to become side tracked and begin talking about other, more interesting topics.

If your study group is not working well together

- Discuss your difficulties and try to resolve them.
- Agree as a group to stop. You do not want to lose good friends.

As the examination date gets closer

- Create a timetable for revising, setting realistic targets. You may need to cancel social events and video favourite TV programmes to watch after the examination.
- Plan which subjects you are going to study. The examination will cover the whole syllabus so it is important that you do not become very familiar with the first section and never revise the last section.
- Find a good time to revise and a suitable place. Remember that everyone studies in a different way.
- Ask your tutor for guidance on any subject areas you do not understand. You will remember information more clearly if you understand it.
- Go to any revision tutorials that are provided.

The week before the examination:

- check that you know the starting time of the assessment, where it is being held and what equipment you need to take with you.
- Read through all your notes.
- Make sure that your transport and child care facilities are full proof. If you are responsible for dropping off and collecting a child from nursery or school it is important to make alternative arrangements for the day.

The night before the examination

- Try to relax.
- Get a good night's sleep.
- Avoid cramming i.e. trying to store a large quantity of information within a very short space of time. People tend to do this a few days before the examination because they have not planned their time effectively and are running out of time. This is not an effective method of revising and should be avoided if at all possible.

The day of the examination:

- Arrive in plenty of time at the examination centre.
- Talk to your friends but do not be put off if they have revised work that you have not.
- Go into the examination room as soon as possible and spend some time getting yourself organised.

If you have revised well, you will be able to answer the questions confidently.

Plan your time

- When you turn over the question paper, do not panic and start answering the questions straight away.
- Take time to read the paper.
- Decide the order in which you are going to answer the questions.
- Time yourself e.g. you should be able to answer approximately half the questions by half time.
- Plan time to re-read your answers and make alterations if necessary.

Answer the questions

- Do not lose confidence if you cannot answer the first question. Go back to it when you have written a few answers.
- Read the question carefully before answering it. Look at the key instructions and the mark allocations.
- Answer the questions that you are confident about first.

Read your answers

- Take time to read your answers. You may have missed out information.

| **Check that you have answered all the questions** | • Remember that you cannot gain marks if you do not answer a question. It is important to answer every question briefly than provide a very detailed answer to one question which is not asked for. |
| **If you run short of time** | • Write in note form if it is absolutely necessary. (This is not possible in a multiple choice question paper.) |

A C T I V I T Y

Read all the questions through carefully before you start working. You have ten minutes to complete the task, so use a watch to time yourself.

1 Write your name in full.
2 Write your address in the bottom right hand corner of the paper.
3 Draw THREE small circles in the top right hand corner of the paper.
4 Write the name of two footballers on the back of the paper.
5 Put your pencil down and stop writing for ten seconds.
6 Where would you find Disney Land?
7 Name the capital cities of France, United States of America, Germany.
8 Name THREE fruits beginning with the letter A.
9 Raise your hand for ten seconds.
10 Answer only question number one.

Did you answer all the questions? If you did, go back and read the questions again. Remember, it is always very important to read the questions carefully before you begin to write the answers.

After the examination:

• Avoid long discussions with your friends, this can make you feel very depressed if you think you have answered the questions incorrectly
• Treat yourself, you deserve it.

Disasters on the day!

We can never predict what is going to happen on the examination day. It can snow and all the roads are blocked, the train breaks down and you know you are going to be very late, you are not well, your child develops an extremely high temperature and you cannot leave the house ...

If you find yourself in this position:

- Contact the examination centre if at all possible and explain the situation. The awarding body will have procedures that will need to be followed.
- Travel to the centre as quickly as possible, you may be allowed to enter the examination room late.
- Write to the examination centre and explain your circumstances.

5

Giving an Oral Presentation or Taking Part in A Class Discussion

---

The aim of this chapter is to help you:

- prepare for and give an oral presentation
- make an effective contribution to group discussions

The importance of being able to give good presentations

You need to give talks:

- to communicate what you have discovered;
- to obtain feedback;
- to advertise yourself;
- and to better understand things by trying to explain them to others.

When you are working with young children you will need to talk to parents and other professionals. Now is the time to practise.

Eight stages towards an effective presentation

Giving a presentation can be a frightening experience but your anxieties can be reduced if you are well prepared. The eight stages that are outlined below will give you a framework to work towards.

Stage 1   Choose the topic for the presentation

⇩

Stage 2   Research the topic

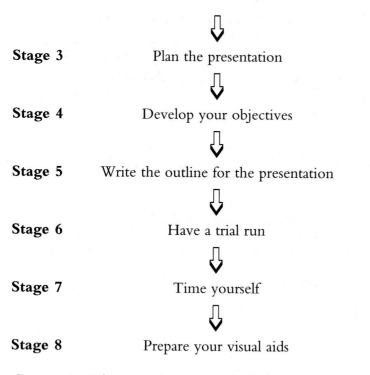

Stage 3	Plan the presentation
Stage 4	Develop your objectives
Stage 5	Write the outline for the presentation
Stage 6	Have a trial run
Stage 7	Time yourself
Stage 8	Prepare your visual aids

Stage 1 Choose the topic for the presentation

If you are allowed to choose the topic always select a subject that you know a lot about as it can help to boost your confidence. If you are not given a choice then you must research your subject really well and take detailed notes.

Stage 2 Research the topic

Finding information for a presentation should be carried out in the same way as you would for an assignment. Visit the Learning Resources Centre, take detailed notes and remember to reference your sources.

Stage 3 Plan your presentation

Before you begin to plan your presentation it is important to know who your audience is going to be and how much they know about the subject you are talking about. If you cannot find out this information assume that they know less rather than more.

Every presentation should have:
a beginning   which explains what the topic is and what your main objectives are going to be
a middle   which explains each of your aims

an end   which provides a brief summary of what you have said

It is always helpful to decide what your objectives are as they can provide a framework for your presentation e.g. If you have been asked to give a presentation on how the nursery ensures equality of opportunity your aims may be to:

- explain the meaning of the term 'equality of opportunity;
- give practical examples of how the nursery ensures equality of opportunity;
- explain the role of the adult

Avoid having too many objectives as this can become confusing for the listener.

Stage 4 Develop your objectives

Take each objective in turn and write detailed notes on the information you have gathered. These can be reduced to bullet points when you have gathered all the information you require.

Stage 5 Write the outline of the presentation

When you have been asked to give a presentation, you will not be expected to read your notes word for word. It is therefore very important to write an outline of the presentation. The final result could be written on index cards or overhead transparencies. Power Point is a useful software package, which can be used to create overhead transparencies.

Sean is an early years student who has been asked to give a 5–10 minute presentation on his experiences in his nursery placement.

The objectives that he has chosen are:

- To provide information about the placement.
- To give a brief outline of the daily routine of the placement.
- To share what he has learned from working with the children.

As part of his preparation, he has asked the nursery for a copy of their welcome booklet. The booklet is normally given to each new parent and it provides information on the nursery.

Time	Information to be given	Visual aids
2 minutes	Explain what the purpose of the presentation is and give a brief description of the nursery.	Overhead transparency Nursery booklet
4 minutes	Explain the daily routine of the placement.	Handout with details about the routine. Photographs showing the children participating in specific activities/experiences.
4 minutes	Explain what has been learned from working with the children	Overhead transparency with bullet points highlighting the main experiences.

Sean has planned for the full ten minutes allowed because he knows he will talk much faster during the presentation than he normally would as he will be very nervous. Having completed this brief plan, he is now going to make detailed notes on each section.

Stage 6 Have a trial run!

It is essential to practise your presentation in the privacy of your own home. It is not necessary to have an audience. Sometimes it is more helpful to talk to yourself. Do this several times in order to build up your confidence.

Stage 7 Time yourself

When you are asked to give a presentation, you are usually given a time limit. It is very important that your talk is within the limit. If you overrun you are often asked to stop and as a result some of the information you wanted to give is left out. This could result in you losing marks if the presentation is being assessed. Equally you may be penalised if the presentation is too short. When you are timing yourself allow time for nerves on the day because you will automatically talk faster.

Stage 8 Prepare your visual aids

Visual aids can enhance the quality of the presentation if they are relevant and can be seen clearly by the audience. Visual aids may include:

- illustrations
- equipment
- charts
- objects

Using and preparing overhead transparencies

When giving a presentation, overhead transparencies can be used for a variety of different reasons.

- Provide a summary of what you are going to say.
- Keep the interest of the audience.
- Act as a reminder for you of what you want to say.

However it is important to ask yourself before you begin to prepare your overhead acetates why are you using them. It may be more appropriate to use other types of visual aid.

On average you should use no more than seven transparencies for every 10 minutes of presentation.

Always word-process your transparencies rather than hand writing them particularly, if you are using them for a presentation that is being assessed. It is essential that the transparency is clear and legible.

A) FONT

It is worth spending some time experimenting with the different fonts on your soft ware package to see which one is the most effective for transparencies.

B) PRINT SIZE

The size of the print on a transparency is very important. If it is too small no one will be able to read it. If it is too large you will have to use too many transparencies for your presentation and you can lose the attention of your audience.

C) USE OF COLOUR

Colour on a transparency can be very effective or it can be disastrous. Some light colours are impossible to see while some dark colours are so dark that you cannot read them. It is essential that you not only experiment on your word processor but you also try out different colours using the overhead projector.

D) NUMBER OF WORDS ON THE OVERHEAD TRANSPARENCY

Avoid the temptation to write your script on the transparency, as this is not what they are designed for. Summarise the main points and highlight them by using bullet points or numbering.

E) LOWER CASE AND CAPITAL LETTERS

Some presenters use capital letters throughout their transparencies. This can be extremely difficult for any members of your audience who have a reading difficulty. It is more appropriate to use capital letters at the beginning of each statement and lower case letters for the remainder of the text.

ACTIVITY

Word process the information below. Highlight the text and click on **bold**. (An easy way to do this is to press Ctrl + B.) Alter the font and print size. When you have found a font and print size that you like, print off your work and make a note of the details.

When preparing overhead acetates you need to consider

- the font style
- the size of the print
- whether or not to use colour
- the number of words on your acetate.

This can take some time but once you have found what you like you will be able to use it each time your prepare acetates.

Giving the presentation

Be prepared

On the day that you are going to give the presentation, make sure that you have your notes, visual aids and transparencies in the order that you are going to use them.

Always check any equipment that you intend using, well in advance of the presentation. If you are using an overhead projector the following checklist may be useful.

The OHP is switched on.

The bulb is working. If it is not you will need to change the OHP or ask for help. You will not be able to put in a new bulb.

The OHP is at an appropriate distance from the screen.

The words on the overhead transparency are in focus. If they are not turn the large black wheel on the arm of the OHP until it comes into focus.

The print is an appropriate size. If it is not move the OHP either towards the screen or away from the screen until it is right.

The person at the back of the room can see the whole of the transparency.

The upright on the OHP is not blocking the view of the audience.

The room is dark enough to see the screen clearly.

It is always useful to give each member of your audience a copy of the transparencies that you are going to use. This is particularly valuable if the overhead projector does not work on the day.

Take your time

Before you begin your presentation it is always worth taking a deep breath to calm your nerves. Try to avoid speaking too quickly and make sure that everyone can hear you. If possible use different intonations in your voice to maintain interest.

Keep an eye on your audience

It is very important to watch your audience as you are giving your presentation as it can give you an indication of how well they are listening to you. In order to maintain their interest you should:

- maintain eye contact with your audience. Sometimes it is tempting to focus on a spot on the far away wall but this only results in alienating your audience. They like to feel part of the talk.
- use different facial expressions. Try to remember to smile even if you are nervous.

- move your hands or your position, however do not do it too often as it can become distracting.
- the way you stand can show how confident you are feeling. Never sit on the edge of a table as this is too relaxed for a formal presentation.
- be smart but avoiding wearing clothes that will distract your audience.

Giving a short talk – Key Skills Level 2 Communication

If you have completed each of the eight stages outlined in this chapter then you should be prepared to be assessed on the quality and content of your presentation. Use the checklist below to find out if you are ready or not.

Part A What you need to know

Key Skills criteria	Evidence for your portfolio	Tick each section when you think you have completed the task
1 Prepare for the talk • research the topic	Photocopy of articles used, if possible bibliography of text used notes taken from different sources	
• make notes	Make notes from sources of three pages or more (remember to provide a reference)	
• choose images	The image is suitable for the presentation Design own overhead transparencies, charts, posters etc. Select images from other sources e.g. nursery documentation	

Key Skills criteria	Evidence for your portfolio	Tick each section when you think you have completed the task
2 Adapt your language to suit your subject, purpose and situation • use standard English • avoid or explain technical terms • keep attention by varying tone of voice	Make detailed notes of the talk showing the language that you are going to use Make a list of the technical terms that you are going to use and provide a definition for each Identify in your notes where it would be appropriate to use different tones of voice	
3 Structure what you say to help listeners follow a line of thought or series of event	Provide a plan of the talk which includes aims and objectives Show in your notes where you can use language to help the listener e.g. firstly, secondly and finally	
4 Use images to help others understand the main points of your talk	Indicate in your notes what images you are going to use and if you made them yourself. Explain in your notes how you are going to use the image. Include your image or a photograph of it in your portfolio.	

Now that you have completed your preparation, you are ready to be assessed.

Part B What you need to do

C2.1b **Give a short talk about a straightforward subject using an image.** Your talk must be between 5 and 6 minutes. It will be given to two or three people. The topic will be related to your work, an area of interest or programme of study. Brief notes may be used as prompts but you should not read them out.	• Speak clearly in a way that suits your subject, purpose and situation • Keep to the subject and structure your talk to help listeners follow what your are saying • Use an image to clearly illustrate your main points

Your assessor will be assessing you on your ability to:

- give a clear talk
- provide a well structured talk;
- keep to the point;
- illustrate the main points through the use of at least one image;
- hold the attention of the audience.

Taking part in a discussion

Being able to take part in a discussion is an essential part of an early years practitioner's job. You will be asked to contribute in team meetings, at parent events, during child protection case conferences etc. It is therefore important that you feel build up your confidence during your training.

The purpose of a discussion is to allow a group of people to talk informally about a topic of mutual concern, share experiences, express different opinions and discuss alternatives. Within an early years setting many discussions will result in action plans being developed.

The value of taking part

- Your opinions and observations are valuable. This is particularly true when discussing the progress of an individual child. As an early years student you will have a different relationship with the child and you will observe aspects of the child's behaviour that permanent staff may miss.
- When you are in full time employment you must be able to explain and discuss issues with parents and other professional workers. You gain confidence by practising the skill.
- It can help you think through issues and ultimately learn more about the subject area.

Avoiding taking part in discussions

People avoid saying anything during discussions for a number of reasons.

- They may be very shy.
- They may feel inadequate and that their contribution is going to be seen as silly.
- They can't be bothered taking part possibly because the discussion is not interesting.
- They do not know enough about the subject being discussed.

ACTIVITY

Think back to a time when you had a lively discussion with a group of friends. Did you take part in the discussion? Did you enjoy it? Did you learn anything from it?

Take a few moments to think why you found it easy or difficult to take part in the discussion.

Building up your confidence to take part in a discussion

- Be familiar with the subject area. It is difficult to make a valuable contribution if you do not know anything about the topic.
- Listen to the contribution made by others
- Answer questions during a teaching session.
- Start small – make a conscious effort to take part at least once during a discussion.

Planning your contribution

If you know that a discussion is going to take place, then this gives you the opportunity to prepare beforehand.

- Brainstorm or draw a mind map of the possible topics that may be considered as part of the discussion
- Research the subject area e.g. relevant text books, child's records, government documents
- Make notes on any issues that you are particularly interested in or do not understand
- Write down a few questions that you could ask during the discussion to help it move forward.

ACTIVITY

Your placement supervisor has explained that she is concerned that a three year old child has not settled in well into the nursery. He has been coming to the nursery for six weeks. At the next team meeting she would like everyone to come prepared to discuss the progress that the child is making and suggest possible ways in which the child may be supported.

1 What information do you need to have about the child before the team meeting to ensure that you make a valuable contribution to the discussion?

2 What sources will provide the information you require?

3 As an early years student will you have access to each of the sources? If not, why not?

Discuss this activity with a small group of colleagues.

6

Building a portfolio

The aim of the chapter is to help you

- understand what a portfolio is
- gather evidence for your portfolio.

What is a portfolio?

A portfolio is usually a file or an electronically based storage and retrieval system for collecting evidence of your skills and knowledge. The portfolio is used as a way of gathering evidence for a number of different qualifications including NVQ Level 2, 3 and 4 Early Years Care and Education and Key Skills. Most people use arch lever files to store this information with dividers to separate each section of work.

The evidence that you need to collect in order to achieve your qualification will be described in the information provided by the awarding body. The qualification is usually made up of units and within each unit there will be a number of different criteria. You will need to provide evidence to show that you are competent in all the criteria.

Key Skills and portfolio building

If you are working towards one or more of the mandatory Key Skills units i.e. Communication, Application of Number and Information Technology you will be required to provide evidence for each criterion within Part B. It is important that you read the criteria carefully before you start to gather evidence.

Starting your portfolio

Once you have decided how you are going to store your information it is very important to provide personal details at the beginning of the file.

- Write your name and address clearly at the beginning of the file. (This may be invaluable if you leave your file on the bus!)

- Write the name and level of award or key skills unit that you are working towards.
- If you are working with young children, describe your place of work and the age range of the children you are working with. Do not name the work setting or the staff with whom you work or the name of the child or family. It is important to maintain confidentiality at all times.
- Begin with a contents page. This can be very useful when trying to find specific forms of evidence.
- Use dividers to separate individual units.
- Number the pages of your file. Do not do this until you have completed the whole file.
- Begin to compile a bibliography. Do not be tempted to leave this task until you have gathered all your evidence, as you may not be able to find the original source.
- Include an index at the back of your file. This should show where the evidence requirements have been met. The example below shows how you may do it for Communication.

Portfolio page	Criterion reference	Type of evidence
1	C3.1b	Detailed notes of the presentation
2–6	C3.1b	Overhead transparencies
7–9	C3.1b	Handouts for audience
10	C3.1b	Programme for the presentation showing the sequence in which the information will be given.
11	C3.1b	Video of the presentation

Remember, you're evidence may be very different to the example given above.

Methods of presenting evidence

In order to show that you have the skills to complete a task or you have the knowledge and understanding of the subject area, you are required to provide relevant, valid and authenticated evidence.

The evidence that you provide can be in a variety of different formats.

a) Most of your evidence will be on paper i.e. written material

- Notes taken from text books or other sources
- Observations of children
- Work plans e.g. activities provided for children
- Log books and/or diaries
- Assignments

b) Visual material e.g.

- Photographs of you working with the children
- Art work e.g. children's work that has been produced as a result of an activity you have planned
- Overhead transparencies
- Displays
- Charts, diagrams, graphs
- Videos or audio tapes

c) Physical products e.g.

- Resources you have made to use with the children
- Working models to illustrate how you are going to use them with the children

d) Records from observations of your performance

- Witness statements by your placement supervisor or tutor. This form of evidence cannot be the only form of evidence for some criteria in the Key Skill units.
- Assessor reports on observing you either in the work setting or carrying out simulations.
- Tutor reports e.g. Your ability to take part in a discussion.
- Previous qualifications that have been approved by the awarding body e.g. GCSE certificates.

Gathering evidence for the Key Skills units in Communication, Application of Number and Information Technology

If you are working towards key skills, you can use evidence from any aspect of your experiences and not simply your vocational course e.g.

community work, employment experience, Duke of Edinburgh Award schemes or work placements. However it is likely that most of your evidence will be collected from the work that you complete on your vocational course.

Remember that irrespective of where you take your evidence from, the evidence must be properly authenticated and assessed.

Recording portfolio evidence

When you insert your evidence into your portfolio you should provide as much information as possible. It should include:

- The appropriate criteria number e.g. Part A Communication C2.3
- The purpose of the evidence e.g. 'These notes show that I am able to read and summarise information about the emotional and social development of the child'
- Details of preparation and resources that you have used

Some key skill units give specific detail that must be included in your portfolio. It is very important that you discuss it with your tutor to ensure that you do not miss out any relevant information.

ACTIVITY

When you begin to prepare for an assignment for your early years qualification, use the instructions below to gather evidence for Key Skills Communication and Information Technology.

1 Using the Internet, find the web page of the child-care magazine e.g. Nursery World, Child Education. Make a note of the web address and file it in your portfolio.
2 Find an article in the web site that gives you information on the subject you are studying. Save the article onto a file. Name the file. Print the window to show the name of the file that you are using and file it in your portfolio.
3 Write brief notes to explain the tasks that you have done so far and file them in your portfolio. Ask your key skills tutor to sign your work to state that you completed the work by yourself.
4 Print off a copy of the article that you have chosen and file it in your portfolio.

5 Read the article and make notes of the information that you have read to show that you understand the content. File the notes in your portfolio.

6 In class, discuss the information that you have read, with your tutor by yourself or in a small group. When you are being assessed on your ability to take part in a discussion you will need to show:
   a) that you can outline the main ideas in the article.
   b) that you can speak clearly
   c) how you are going to use the information to help you to write your assignment.
   You will need to ask your tutor to complete and sign a form to state that you have taken an effective role in the discussion. This form should then be put into your portfolio.

7 Using the Learning Resource Centre or your own text-books, find a chapter that refers to the subject that you are working on. Read the chapter and write notes. (One of the text that you use for this assignment must contain an image.) Remember to take a note of the author, date of publication, title of book, place of publishing and publishers name. You should also note the pages that you have read. When you have finished this section, put your notes into your portfolio.

8 You may need to continue your search for information in order to write your assignment. If you have made notes, you could include this additional evidence in your portfolio.

9 Write draft notes for your assignment. On your draft, show how you have checked your spelling, grammar and punctuation. You could do this by writing your corrections above the error. Put this work into your portfolio.

10 When you have finished writing your draft assignment, word-process your work. Put this work into your portfolio. Write brief notes to explain how you checked your work for errors in spelling, grammar and punctuation. Put the accurate copy of the assignment into your portfolio.

When you present your assignment, include your name, unit title and level, page number and date in the header and/or footer. You could also use bold, underlining, colour, bullet points etc. to highlight specific information.

Save your completed assignment onto a file and name the file appropriately. Print off the window to show the file that you are using. Put all of this work into your file.

Having completed this task it is now very important to reference your work against the key skills units.

This activity is similar to the previous one but it relates specifically to Key Skills Application of Number Level 1. Some of the evidence may be used for Information Technology.

As an experienced nanny, you have been asked to plan a week's holiday abroad in May for two children aged five years and eight years of age. You will have sole responsibility for the children during the holiday. You will fly from London Gatwick to a country of your choice. The total cost of the holiday should not exceed £800 and that should include travel insurance for yourself and the children and spending money.

Plan the arrangements for the holiday.

Task 1

Decide on a destination that you feel would be appropriate for the children. Using the Internet, gather as much information as you can on. This should include:

- a table or chart that shows possible flight times;
- a table or chart showing the costs of the holiday at different times in the year;
- details of how much travel insurance will cost.

Download any information that you find and save it in a file. Name the file and print the window showing the file name. Print the information that you have found. Put this work in your portfolio. N1.1

Calculate:
a) the total cost of the holiday for yourself and the two children. Show all your calculations. Remember to include the travel insurance. N1.2a
b) how much spending money you will have. Show all your calculations and include this work in your portfolio. N1.2a
c) what time you need to arrive at the airport assuming that you need to be

their two hours before the flight. Calculate the length of the flight taking account of any time differences. N1.2a

Remember that you must show that you have checked to make sure that your calculations make sense.

Task 2

Using the Learning Resource Centre, find a text-book on the destination that you have chosen. If you can, photocopy the relevant information but make sure that you do not break copyright laws.

Find out what the temperature will be in May and work out the temperature mean and range of the country over the year. Show all the calculations that you made and explain how you checked the results to make sure they made sense and include all your work in your portfolio. N1.2c

Task 3

Choose a suitable way to present your findings to the children's parent. You must use a chart and a diagram and it may be word-processed. N1.3

You will need to:

Show how the results of your calculations relate to the purpose of the task.

You may find that it is not possible to show all the criteria in Part B in one piece of work. You will then need to provide additional evidence for these sections.

Assessing your portfolio

When you have completed your portfolio it will be assessed by your key skills tutor or NVQ assessor. When he/she is satisfied that the work is sufficient, valid and reliable it will then be presented for internal verification. An external verifier will then visit the centre and he/she may want to look at your portfolio and perhaps ask you some questions about the work you have done.

Top Ten Tips

Avoid the ten traps of studying

1 'I don't know where to begin'

Take control. Make a list of what you need to do. Break down your work into manageable chunks. Set yourself realistic targets. Do not miss classes. Use any spare time effectively. Reward yourself when you achieve your goals.

2 'I've got so much to study and not enough time do it in'

Look quickly over the syllabus and your notes. Find the topics that you do not understand and the areas that have been emphasised by your tutor. Concentrate on those areas.

3 'This is so boring. I can't stay awake when I am reading it'

Wake up! Get involve in the materials. Take notes. Underline key words. Use the PSQ5R method of reading text. Talk to your friends about it (but do not get side tracked).

4 'I read it. I understand it but I just can't get it to sink in'

You are more likely to remember information if you understand it. Try to relate what you are reading to practical examples from your work placement. Use techniques such a mnemonics.

5 'I think I understand it'

Test yourself to make sure. Make up questions and try them out. Ask your friend to test you.

6 'There is too much to remember'

Get organised. Put your notes on to post-its or index cards. Use every available moment to study e.g. train journey. Group the information into categories. Draw mind maps to summarise the information.

7 'I knew it a minute ago'

Keep going back over the topics. Vary the order of your revision pattern. Do not always start at the beginning because you will never reach the end! The more time you spend studying, the more you will remember and understand.

8 'But I like to study in bed'

Research has shown that the greater the similarity between the study setting and the test setting, the greater likelihood that the material studied will be remembered in the examination. Besides, you might fall asleep!

9 'Cramming before an examination helps keep it fresh in my mind'

Study as you go along. You will remember more.

10 'I'm going to stay up all night until I understand this'

Not a good idea. It is important to have short breaks during your study time. If you are exhausted you will not do well in the examination.

Adapted from 'Ten traps of studying'
www.unc.edu/depts/ucc/tentraps.html

Bibliography

Bruce, T. and Meggitt, C. (1999). *Child Care and Education* 2nd Edn. London: Hodder and Stoughton.

Jensen, Eric (1995) *Brain Based Learning and Teaching*. Turning Point.

Lindon, J. (1998) *Child Protection and Early Years Work*. London: Hodder and Stoughton.

Meggitt, C., Stevens, J. and Bruce, T. (2000) *Introduction to Child Care and Education*. London: Hodder and Stoughton.

O'Hagan, M. (1997) *Geraghty's Caring for Young Children*. London: Balliere Tindall.

Rose, C. and Nicholl, M. (1998) *Accelerated Learning for the 21st Century*. London: Piatkus.

Smith, Andrew (1998) *Accelerated learning in the Classroom*. Stafford: Network Educational Press Ltd.

Resources

(The addresses of the early years organisations were correct at time of going to press.)

Association of Advisors for the Under-Eights and their Families
C/o Highclear,
Cot Lane
Chidham
Chichester
Bucks
PO18 8SP

Child Line
2nd Floor
Royal Mail Buildings
Studd Street
London
N1 0QW

Children in Scotland
Princes House
5 Shandwick Place
Edinburgh
EH2 4RG

Children in Wales
25 Windsor Place
Cardiff
CF1 3BZ

Council for Awards in Children's Care and Education
8 Chequer Street
St Albans
AL1 3XZ

Day Care Trust
Shoreditch Town Hall Annexe
380 Old Street
London
EC1V 9LT

Early Education (BAECE)
136 Cavell Street
London

Early Years National Training Organisation
Pilgrims Lodge
5A Holywell Hill
St Albans
AL1 1ER

Early Years Trainers Anti-Racist Network (EYTARN)
PO Box 1870
London
N12 8JO

HomeStart UK
2 Salisbury Road
Leicester
LE1 7QR

Kids Club Network
Bellerive House
3 Muirfield Crescent
London
E14 9SZ

Kidscape
152 Buckingham Palace Road
London
SW10 9TR

National Association for Primary Education (NAPE)
University Centre
Barrack Road
Northampton
NN2 6AF

National Campaign for Nursery Education
Honorary Secretary
BCM Box 6216
London
WC1N 3XX
Publications include:
'The importance of the Local Authority Nursery School'
'Four year olds in reception classes'
'When should your child start school?'
'What do we mean by nursery education?'

National Childminding Association
8 Masons Hall
Bromley
Kent
BR2 9EY

National Children's Bureau
8 Wakely Street
London
EC1V 7QE

National Council of Voluntary Child Care Organisations
Unit 4 Pride Court
80/82 White Lion Street
London
N1 9PF

National Day Nursery Association
16 New North Parade
Huddersfield
HD1 5JP

National Early Years Network
77 Holloway Road
London
N7 8JZ

National Playbus Association
93 Whitby Road
Brislington
Bristol
BS4 3QF

National Society for the Prevention of Cruelty to Children
National Centre
42 Curtain Road
London
EC2A 3NH

NIPPA – The Early Years Organisation
6c Wildflower Way
Apollo Road
Belfast
BT12 6TA

Pre-School Learning Alliance
69 Kings Cross Road
London
WC1X 9LL

Qualification, Curriculum and Assessment Authority (QCA)
29 Bolton Street
London
W1Y 7PD

Qualifications, Curriculum and Assessment Authority for Wales (ACCAC)
Castle Buildings
Womanby Street
Cardiff
CF1 9SX

Save the Children
17 Grove Lane
London
SE5 8RD

Scottish Pre-School Play Association
14 Elliot Place
Glasgow
G3 8EP

Scottish Qualifications Authority (SQA)
Hanover House
24 Douglas Street
Glasgow
G2 7NQ

The Children's Society
Edward Rudolf House
Margery Street
London
WC1X 0JL

The Education Network
1-5 Bath Street
London
EC1V 9QC

The Department of Child Development and Primary Education
Institute of Education
University of London
20 Bedford Way
London
WC1H 0LA

Welsh Office Education Department
Cathays Park
Cardiff
CF1 3NQ

Welsh Pre-school Play Group Association
2a Chester Street
Wrexham
LL13 8BD